The Reach That Restores Christ Love For The Broken

Joshua Rhoades

Published by Joshua Paul Rhoades, 2024.

THE REACH THAT RESTORES CHRIST LOVE FOR THE BROKEN

First edition. October 22, 2024.

Copyright © 2024 Joshua Rhoades.

ISBN: 979-8227131027

Written by Joshua Rhoades.

Also by Joshua Rhoades

Courage Under Fire: David's Stand On The Battlefield
Jonah's Journey: Voices Of Redemption And Lessons In Obedience
The Furnace Of Faith: 12 Principles From The Heat Of Faith
Whispers of Hope: Inspiring Stories of Men's Prayers In Scripture
Frontier Legends: The Oregon Dream
Elijah: A Beacon Of Boldness
HOOK, LINE & SAVIOUR - Faith Reflections from Fishing
Driven By Faith: Motor Racing Inspired Christian Life
30 Day Devotional - Bold and Strong- Coffee Devotions for a Courageous
Christian Walk
Authentic Christianity: The Heart of Old Time Religion
Consider The Ant - God's Tiny Preachers
Flee Fornication: The Plea For Purity
Renewed Hope- How to Find Encouragement in God
Sounding The Call - The Voice of Conviction
The Altar - Where Heaven Meets Earth
The Bible's Battlefields- Timeless Lessons from Ancient Wars
The Sacred Art of Silence - How Silence Speaks in Scripture
Under Fire- The Sanctity of the Traditional Biblical Home
Who Is on the Lord's Side? A Call to Righteousness
What Is Truth? - From Skepticism to Submission
First and Goal- Faith and Football Fundamentals
From Dugout to Devotion- Spiritual Lessons from Baseball
Par for the Course- Faith and Fairways
The Believer's Pace- Tools for Running Life's Marathon
The Immutable Fortress- Security in God's Unchanging Nature
Biblical Bravery
Deer Stands and Devotions: A Hunter's Walk with God

Jesus Knows- Our Hearts, Our Responsibility
Restoration - Setting The Bone
Spiritual 911- God's Word for Life's Emergency's
The Freedom of Forgiveness
The Jezebel Effect - Ancient Manipulations Modern Lessons
The Shout That Stopped The Saviour
The Time Machine Chronicles: Old Testament Characters
Anchored In Truth Exploring The Depths of Psalm 119
Biblical Counsel on Anger
Proverbs' Portraits The Men God Mentions
Stumbling in the Dark - The Dangers of Alcohol
Guarding the Wicket Protecting Your Faith and Game
The Champion's Faith - Wrestling and Achieving Spiritual Victory
Scriptural Commands for Modern Times Living God's Word Today Volume 1
Scriptural Commands for Modern Times Living God's Word Today Volume 2
Scriptural Commands for Modern Times Living God's Word TodayVolume3
The Greatest Gift
A Christmas Journey of Faith
Daughter Of The King: Embracing Your Identity In Christ
Determination and Dedication Building Strong Faith As A Young Man
Walking Through Walls God's Power to Part the Storms of Life
David's Song Of Deliverance Praising God Through Every Storm
From Weakness to Warrior: Gideon's Transformation
Why Did Jesus Weep?
Living For God The Call To Be A Living Sacrifice
My Mind Is In A Fog What Do I Do?
Turning The Page Written By Grace
The Calling and Greatness of John the Baptist
For Such a Time Esther's Courageous Stand
From Brokenness To Beauty Written By The Pen of Grace
The Ultimate Guide to Massive Action- From Plans to Reality
A Heart Of Conviction
Serving In The Shadows
Repentance Revealed The Road Back To God
The Chief Sinner Meets The Chief Saviour Reflections On I Timothy 1:15

Answer The Call - 31 Days of Biblical Action
The Birthmark of the Believer
Reflections on Calvary's Cross
The Kingdom Builder Paul's Bold Proclamation of Christ
The Animal Of Pride
The Reach That Restores Christ Love For The Broken

Dedication

To you, dear reader—this book is for you.

If you have ever felt broken, lost, or burdened by the weight of life, know that you are not alone. This journey you are on, with all its trials, heartaches, and unanswered questions, is one that countless others have walked. And though it may feel like you are too far gone or too wounded to ever find healing, I want you to know that there is a love that reaches even the deepest corners of your soul—a love that restores, renews, and never lets go.

This book is dedicated to the part of you that has struggled, the part that has cried out in the quiet moments when no one else was there to hear. It is dedicated to the part of you that has questioned whether you are truly seen, valued, or known. Jesus sees you. His love is not distant or conditional. He does not wait for you to be perfect, to have it all together, or to be worthy by the world's standards. His love reaches out to you exactly as you are—in your brokenness, in your fear, and in your pain.

Through these pages, my prayer is that you will discover the depth of Christ's love for you, a love that can heal the wounds you thought were beyond repair. I pray that you will encounter the tenderness of His grace, the strength of His hands that lift you when you feel you cannot stand, and the peace of His presence that quiets every storm in your heart. This book is a reminder that no one is beyond the reach of His love, and no brokenness is beyond the power of His restoration.

May these words speak to the parts of your heart that need healing, and may they guide you toward the One who longs to restore you. You are worthy of His love, not because of anything you have done, but because He loves you beyond measure. There is nothing too broken that He cannot make whole. There is nothing too lost that He cannot find.

So, to you, the reader who has walked through pain, I dedicate this book. You are not alone. You are not forgotten. The love of Christ reaches for you even now, and His reach restores. May you find healing, hope, and peace in His arms. This is your story of restoration, and I am honored to walk a small part of it with you through these words.

Introduction

There is a deep ache in the human soul—a yearning for healing, for restoration, for love that doesn't falter in the face of our frailty. In our journey through life, we encounter brokenness in various forms. Some of us carry the wounds of rejection, the scars of past mistakes, or the heavy burden of guilt that lingers even after the moment of failure has passed. Others wrestle with silent grief, hidden sorrows, or the crushing weight of despair when dreams have shattered and hope feels out of reach. Yet, in the midst of all this, there is a truth that transcends every heartache: the love of Christ reaches even the most broken places within us.

This book is a testimony to the power of that love—a love so vast, so unrelenting, that it cannot be hindered by our imperfections, fears, or failures. The love of Christ does not shy away from our brokenness; rather, it draws nearer, pursuing us with a tenderness that transforms. Whether we feel unworthy, too far gone, or too damaged to be restored, His reach extends into the depths of our souls, gently mending what has been torn apart.

In "The Reach That Restores: Christ's Love for the Broken," we explore the profound reality of a Saviour who is not content to leave us as we are. Jesus Christ, the Good Shepherd, seeks out the lost and the brokenhearted with a love that heals. His grace is not reserved for those who have it all together, nor for those whose lives seem unblemished by hardship. Rather, His heart beats for the broken—for those who are weary, wounded, and desperately in need of a touch from the One who makes all things new.

The Bible is rich with stories of restoration—stories that reveal the compassionate reach of a God who binds up the wounds of His people. From the woman caught in adultery, whom Jesus forgave and freed from condemnation, to Peter, who after denying Christ, was lovingly restored to a place of purpose and leadership, we see time and again how Jesus meets people at their lowest points and lifts them up. He does not merely offer second chances—He offers new life, a complete transformation, and a hope that no amount of brokenness can steal.

Perhaps you find yourself in a season where brokenness feels like your constant companion. Perhaps you've believed the lie that your failures or hurts have placed you beyond the reach of God's love. Or maybe you're carrying wounds that no one else can see, yet they ache in the quiet moments of your heart. Wherever you are, know this: Jesus sees you. He knows your pain, and He is already extending His hand toward you with healing in His heart.

This book is an invitation to experience the fullness of Christ's restorative love. Each chapter will guide you through different facets of His healing power—whether it's healing from past hurts, restoring relationships, redeeming what's been lost, or rebuilding hope in the midst of despair. We'll look closely at how His love transcends time, distance, and even our own resistance to reach us in the exact place where we need Him most.

The love of Christ is not passive. It is an active, pursuing love that does not wait for us to make the first move. He reaches out to us in our brokenness, offering a restoration that is far greater than any human effort could achieve. This is not a mere patching up of our wounds, but a complete renewal—a remaking of our hearts, minds, and spirits. His love is one that rebuilds the ruins, restores what has been stolen, and revives the dreams that have been buried under the weight of disappointment.

Throughout the pages of this book, you will encounter stories of those who have experienced this reach that restores. You'll hear from individuals who have walked through seasons of deep loss, shame, and pain, only to find that Christ's love was waiting for them on the other side of their brokenness. Their stories are not just testimonies of survival, but of redemption—of being brought back to life by the touch of the Saviour.

And this restoration is not reserved for a select few. It is for everyone—for every person who has ever felt the sting of rejection, the heaviness of guilt, or the weight of sorrow. No one is too far gone, and no one is beyond the reach of the Saviour's love. He invites all of us to come, to lay down our burdens, and to be restored by His grace.

As you read, I pray that you will feel the warmth of His love drawing near to you. I pray that you will see, perhaps for the first time, that your brokenness is not the end of your story. In fact, it may be the very place where your healing begins. Christ specializes in taking what the world discards and turning it into something beautiful. Your scars, your pain, your failures—none of them are wasted in the hands of the Redeemer.

So, take heart. There is hope. No matter where you've been or what you've gone through, Christ's love is reaching for you even now. His reach is not limited by your past, your circumstances, or your failures. It is a reach that restores, that heals, and that brings new life.

In the pages that follow, may you encounter the depth of His love in a way that transforms you from the inside out. May you discover that His reach truly does restore the broken, and may you find healing, hope, and wholeness in the arms of the One who loves you more than you can imagine.

Welcome to "The Reach That Restores." The journey of restoration begins here.

Chapter 1 - The Savior reaches into the deepest valleys of despair to bring hope.

The Savior reaches into the deepest valleys of despair to bring hope, and there is no depth too dark, no place too low, where His love cannot reach. When life feels overwhelming, when our hearts are broken, and when hope seems lost, the Savior steps in with His gentle, yet powerful hand to lift us out of our despair. He is near to the brokenhearted, and He saves those who are crushed in spirit, as Psalm 34:18 tells us: "The LORD is nigh unto them that are of a broken heart; and saveth such as be of a contrite spirit." This means that in the moments when we feel abandoned, alone, and too weak to carry on, He is not far from us. He is closer than ever, ready to bind our wounds, to bring comfort to our aching hearts, and to give us the strength we need to keep going. The valleys of life, where fear, anxiety, and sorrow can seem unbearable, are the very places where His grace shines the brightest. It is in these valleys that we truly discover the depths of His love, a love that never lets us go, no matter how deep we fall. The Savior doesn't stand at a distance, waiting for us to climb out of the pit ourselves. He enters into our despair with us, walking through the dark places, holding our hand, and guiding us step by step toward the light of hope.

In these moments of despair, when everything seems hopeless, the Savior reminds us that there is always hope in Him. His presence brings light into the darkness. His words bring peace to the troubled soul. He speaks softly to our hearts, "Fear not, for I am with thee," as it says in Isaiah 41:10, "be not dismayed; for I am thy God: I will strengthen thee; yea, I will help thee; yea, I will uphold thee with the right hand of my righteousness." This promise is not just words on a page; it is the very foundation of the hope we cling to in our darkest times. The Savior doesn't just promise to be with us in the good times; He promises to be with us in the worst moments of our lives. When we are in the deepest valleys, He is there, walking beside us, sometimes even carrying us when we can no longer stand on our own. His strength becomes our strength, His peace becomes our peace, and His hope becomes our hope.

The Savior's reach is not limited by our circumstances, our failures, or our doubts. Even when we feel unworthy, even when we have made mistakes that we think cannot be forgiven, His grace is still there, reaching out to us. As Psalm 40:2 declares, "He brought me up also out of an horrible pit, out of the miry clay, and set my feet upon a rock, and established my goings." This is what the Savior does for us when we are trapped in despair. He lifts us out of the pit, cleanses us from the dirt of our failures, and sets us on solid ground. He gives us a new beginning, a fresh start, and the assurance that we are loved and valued by Him. In His hands, our brokenness is not something to be ashamed of, but something He can use to create beauty. Our scars become a testimony of His healing power and His unwavering faithfulness.

When we are in the valley of despair, it is easy to believe the lie that we are alone, that no one understands our pain, or that no one cares. But the Savior reminds us that He knows our pain intimately. He Himself walked through the darkest valley when He bore the weight of the world's sins on the cross. As Isaiah 53:3-4 says, "He is despised and rejected of men; a man of sorrows, and acquainted with grief: and we hid as it were our faces from him; he was despised, and we esteemed him not. Surely he hath borne our griefs, and carried our sorrows." Jesus understands despair because He has experienced it firsthand. He took on our suffering so that we would never have to walk through the valley alone. Because of this, we can trust that He knows how to comfort us, how to heal us, and how to bring hope to the most hopeless situations.

The Savior's hope is not just a fleeting feeling or an empty promise. It is a living hope, grounded in His resurrection power. As 1 Peter 1:3 proclaims, "Blessed be the God and Father of our Lord Jesus Christ, which according to his abundant mercy hath begotten us again unto a lively hope by the resurrection of Jesus Christ from the dead." This living hope is what sustains us in the valley of despair. It reminds us that no matter how dark things may seem, there is always the promise of new life, new beginnings, and new joy in Christ. The same power that raised Jesus from the dead is the power that lifts us out of our despair and gives us the strength to face tomorrow. This hope is not dependent on our circumstances, but on the unchanging character of God. It is a hope that cannot be shaken, because it is anchored in the truth that Jesus has already overcome the world (John 16:33).

In the valley, the Savior calls us to trust in Him, even when we cannot see the way out. Proverbs 3:5-6 encourages us, "Trust in the LORD with all thine heart; and lean not unto thine own understanding. In all thy ways acknowledge him, and he shall direct thy paths." Trusting in the Savior means believing that He is working, even when we don't understand what He is doing. It means surrendering our need to control the situation and allowing Him to lead us, step by step, toward the hope and future He has promised. This trust is not always easy, especially when the valley seems long and the darkness overwhelming, but it is in these moments of trust that we experience the peace that surpasses all understanding (Philippians 4:7).

The Savior's reach into the valley of despair also reminds us of His relentless pursuit of us. Even when we try to run from Him, even when we feel unworthy of His love, He comes after us, seeking us out like the shepherd who leaves the ninety-nine to find the one lost sheep. As Luke 15:4-5 tells us, "What man of you, having an hundred sheep, if he lose one of them, doth not leave the ninety and nine in the wilderness, and go after that which is lost, until he find it? And when he hath found it, he layeth it on his shoulders, rejoicing." The Savior rejoices when He finds us in the valley and carries us back to safety on His shoulders. His love is not conditional on our performance; it is unconditional, never-ending, and always seeking to bring us back to Him.

Even in the valley, the Savior is working all things for our good. Romans 8:28 assures us, "And we know that all things work together for good to them that love God, to them who are the called according to his purpose." This doesn't mean that the valley itself is good, but that the Savior can use even our darkest moments to bring about something beautiful. He can take our pain and turn it into purpose. He can take our sorrow and turn it into joy. He can take our despair and turn it into hope. This is the power of the Savior's reach—nothing is wasted in His hands. Every tear, every heartache, every trial is used by Him to draw us closer to His heart and to shape us into the people He created us to be.

In the end, the Savior's reach into the deepest valleys of despair is a reminder that we are never alone, never forgotten, and never beyond the reach of His love. No matter how low we feel, no matter how hopeless our situation seems, the Savior is there, ready to lift us up, to heal our hearts, and to fill us with His hope. As Psalm 46:1 says, "God is our refuge and strength, a very present help in trouble." The Savior is our refuge, our safe place, and our constant source of hope in every season of life. In His arms, we find the strength to keep going, the peace to calm our anxious hearts, and the hope that shines brightly, even in the darkest valleys.

Chapter 2 - The Savior reaches across every nation and culture to offer salvation.

The Savior reaches across every nation and culture to offer salvation, extending His loving arms to every corner of the world, to every person, no matter who they are or where they come from. His love knows no boundaries, and His desire is that all would come to know Him and receive the gift of salvation. The Bible reminds us in John 3:16, "For God so loved the world, that he gave his only begotten Son, that whosoever believeth in him should not perish, but have everlasting life." The Savior's reach is universal; it is not limited by language, race, or geography. His heart is for every person in every nation, and He offers the same promise to all: the promise of eternal life through belief in Him. His love and salvation are not exclusive to a specific group, but are available to "whosoever" believes. This means that no matter where we are born, what language we speak, or what our background is, the Savior's offer of salvation is for us. It's for the poor and the rich, the young and the old, the educated and the uneducated. The Savior doesn't care about our status or our nationality—He cares about our hearts.

When we look at the Savior's life and ministry, we see Him reaching out to people from all walks of life, from different regions and cultures. In Matthew 28:19, He commanded His disciples to "Go ye therefore, and teach all nations, baptizing them in the name of the Father, and of the Son, and of the Holy Ghost." This was a clear instruction to spread the message of salvation to all nations, not just to the people of Israel, but to the whole world. The Savior's salvation is for every nation because His love is boundless. He desires that no one should be left out. The command to go and make disciples of all nations is a reflection of God's heart—a heart that yearns for every person, from every tribe and tongue, to know Him. It doesn't matter what our cultural background is; God wants us to be part of His family. In Acts 10:34-35, Peter acknowledges this when he says, "Of a truth I perceive that God is no respecter of persons: But in every nation he that feareth him, and worketh righteousness, is accepted with him." God does not show favoritism. He does not prefer one nation over another, nor does He love one culture more than another. His love is equal and abundant for every human being on earth.

The beauty of the Savior's reach is that it breaks down all barriers that humans have built. In a world where divisions exist—whether they are racial, cultural, economic, or social—the Savior brings unity. Galatians 3:28 tells us, "There is neither Jew nor Greek, there is neither bond nor free, there is neither male nor female: for ye are all one in Christ Jesus." In Christ, all the distinctions that often divide us are erased. We are one in Him, and His salvation brings us together as brothers and sisters. When the Savior reaches across every nation and culture, He does so to bring people into a united family, a family that is built on love, grace, and the truth of the Gospel. His love transcends borders, and His salvation is the great equalizer, making no distinction between people. Whether you are from a small village in a remote country or from a bustling city, the Savior's hand is stretched out to you with the same offer of grace and redemption.

The Savior's reach across every nation and culture is also a reminder that His kingdom is not of this world, but it is a kingdom that includes people from every nation, tribe, and language. Revelation 7:9 paints a beautiful picture of this: "After this I beheld, and, lo, a great multitude, which no man could number, of all nations, and kindreds, and people, and tongues, stood before the throne, and before the Lamb, clothed with white robes, and palms in their hands." In heaven, there will be a multitude of people from every nation, worshiping together before the throne of God. This is the ultimate fulfillment of the Savior's reach across the world—bringing together a diverse group of people, united by their faith in Jesus Christ. The Savior's heart is for every single person, and He will not stop until His message of salvation has reached every corner of the earth. His love compels us to share the good news with others, to go into the world and spread His message of hope and redemption, because He desires that all would be saved (1 Timothy 2:4).

Throughout the Bible, we see countless examples of the Savior's reach extending to people from different nations and cultures. One powerful story is that of the Samaritan woman at the well in John 4. In those days, Jews and

Samaritans did not associate with each other, and there were deep cultural divisions between the two groups. But Jesus broke through these barriers when He spoke to the Samaritan woman and offered her living water—eternal life. This shows us that the Savior is not limited by societal norms or prejudices. He reaches out to people regardless of what others think or say. His love crosses all barriers, and He offers salvation to everyone, no matter their past or where they come from. When the Samaritan woman received His message, she went and shared it with her whole town, and many came to believe in Jesus because of her testimony. This is the power of the Savior's reach—it not only changes individual lives, but it spreads to entire communities and nations.

The Savior's reach also extends to those who may feel far from Him because of their background, beliefs, or experiences. Ephesians 2:13 says, "But now in Christ Jesus ye who sometimes were far off are made nigh by the blood of Christ." No one is too far from the reach of the Savior. His sacrifice on the cross made it possible for all people, no matter how far they have wandered, to be brought near to God. The blood of Christ bridges the gap between us and God, and it bridges the gaps between different people groups. The Savior's reach is not hindered by distance, by cultural differences, or by human sin. His blood has made a way for all to come to Him and be saved.

The message of salvation is not just for one group of people—it is for the entire world. This is why the Savior sends out His followers to spread the Gospel to every nation. Romans 10:13-15 tells us, "For whosoever shall call upon the name of the Lord shall be saved. How then shall they call on him in whom they have not believed? And how shall they believe in him of whom they have not heard? And how shall they hear without a preacher? And how shall they preach, except they be sent?" The Savior's reach extends through His followers, who are called to go and tell others about the salvation He offers. We are His hands and feet, bringing His message of love and redemption to people who have never heard it. Every nation and culture needs to hear the Gospel, and the Savior empowers His people to carry this message to the ends of the earth.

One of the most beautiful aspects of the Savior's reach across every nation and culture is that He values and honors the unique differences in each one. He doesn't erase our individuality or our cultural identities, but He redeems them. When we come to Christ, we bring our whole selves—our backgrounds, our experiences, our cultures—and He uses them for His glory. In His kingdom, there is beauty in diversity, and every culture has something to offer in worship and service to Him. The Savior's reach doesn't make us all the same; it unites us in our diversity, making us one body with many parts, as 1 Corinthians 12:12-14 explains: "For as the body is one, and hath many members, and all the members of that one body, being many, are one body: so also is Christ. For by one Spirit are we all baptized into one body, whether we be Jews or Gentiles, whether we be bond or free; and have been all made to drink into one Spirit."

In conclusion, the Savior's reach across every nation and culture to offer salvation is a powerful reminder of His boundless love and grace. He is not limited by borders or divisions; His salvation is for everyone. From the beginning of time, His heart has been for the nations, and His desire is that all would come to know Him and receive the gift of eternal life. No one is excluded from His reach, and His arms are open wide to all who will come to Him. As followers of Christ, we are called to be part of His mission, to share the message of salvation with the world, knowing that His love is for every person, in every nation, in every culture. The Savior's reach is global, it is personal, and it is eternal, offering hope and redemption to all who believe.

Chapter 3 - The Savior reaches into broken hearts to bring healing and restoration.

The Savior reaches into broken hearts to bring healing and restoration, and there is no pain too deep or wound too great for Him to heal. When life's troubles overwhelm us, when we feel shattered and unable to pick up the pieces of our lives, the Savior is there, tenderly reaching out to us, offering His love and His power to restore what has been broken. He sees the pain that others cannot see, and He knows the burdens we carry in the quiet moments when we feel most alone. Psalm 147:3 tells us, "He healeth the broken in heart, and bindeth up their wounds." This is the heart of the Savior—to bring healing to those who are hurting, to comfort those who are mourning, and to restore hope to those who feel lost. His touch is gentle, but it is powerful. He does not leave us in our brokenness, but He works in our hearts, mending the pieces that we thought could never be whole again. No matter how deep the hurt, no matter how long the suffering has lasted, the Savior's healing is always enough. He is the great physician, the healer of our souls, and He lovingly binds up every wound with the care and compassion of a loving Savior.

In the moments when our hearts are broken, it can feel as though the pain will never end. The weight of grief, loss, disappointment, or betrayal can be crushing, and it's easy to feel like we will never be the same again. But the Savior's promise is that He is close to us in these moments. Psalm 34:18 assures us, "The LORD is nigh unto them that are of a broken heart; and saveth such as be of a contrite spirit." The Savior does not watch from a distance when we are hurting; He draws near to us. He enters into our pain with us, and His presence brings comfort and peace that goes beyond our understanding. He understands what it means to have a broken heart, for He, too, experienced sorrow and grief. Isaiah 53:3 describes Jesus as "a man of sorrows, and acquainted with grief." He knows the depths of human suffering, and because of this, He is able to comfort us in a way that no one else can. When our hearts are breaking, we can rest in the knowledge that the Savior knows our pain, and He is with us in the midst of it, offering His comfort and His healing touch.

The Savior's healing is not just about making us feel better in the moment—it is about true restoration. He doesn't just patch up the broken pieces of our hearts; He makes us whole again. Ezekiel 36:26 declares, "A new heart also will I give you, and a new spirit will I put within you: and I will take away the stony heart out of your flesh, and I will give you an heart of flesh." The Savior's healing goes deep. It transforms us from the inside out, giving us a new heart that is soft, responsive, and open to His love. When our hearts have been hardened by pain, when we've built walls around ourselves to protect us from further hurt, the Savior gently breaks down those barriers and gives us a heart that is tender and full of His grace. His restoration is complete. He doesn't just heal us halfway or leave us with scars that continue to cause us pain. He brings complete healing, restoring us to the fullness of life that He desires for us.

When we think about the Savior's reach into broken hearts, we are reminded of the story of Jesus healing the brokenhearted in His ministry. One of the most powerful examples is found in Luke 7, where a sinful woman came to Jesus while He was at the house of Simon the Pharisee. This woman, broken by her sins and the judgment of others, came to Jesus weeping, washing His feet with her tears and wiping them with her hair. She poured out her heart in repentance, and in return, Jesus offered her forgiveness, healing, and restoration. He said to her, "Thy sins are forgiven...Thy faith hath saved thee; go in peace" (Luke 7:48, 50). In this moment, the Savior reached into her brokenness and offered her the peace and healing she so desperately needed. This is what the Savior does for us—He reaches into the places of our hearts that are weighed down by guilt, shame, or sorrow, and He offers us His peace. He tells us to go in peace, knowing that our sins are forgiven and that we have been made new in Him.

Sometimes, the brokenness we experience is not caused by our own actions, but by the actions of others. Betrayal, rejection, and loss can leave us feeling crushed and abandoned. But even in these moments, the Savior's healing is available. In Psalm 147:3, we are reminded again, "He healeth the broken in heart, and bindeth up their wounds." The Savior is not only concerned with our spiritual healing, but He also cares about the emotional wounds we carry. He binds up our wounds like a skilled physician, tenderly caring for us until we are whole again. His healing is a process, and sometimes it takes time, but He is faithful to complete the work He has begun in us. Philippians 1:6 promises, "Being confident of this very thing, that he which hath begun a good work in you will perform it until the day of Jesus Christ." The Savior is committed to our healing and restoration, and He will not stop working in our hearts until we are fully healed.

One of the most beautiful aspects of the Savior's healing is that it is not limited by the depth of our brokenness. There is no heart too broken, no soul too wounded, that the Savior cannot heal. Whether our brokenness comes from past mistakes, present struggles, or the pain others have inflicted on us, the Savior's reach is always enough. His grace is sufficient, as 2 Corinthians 12:9 reminds us: "And he said unto me, My grace is sufficient for thee: for my strength is made perfect in weakness." In our weakest moments, when we feel like we cannot go on, the Savior's strength is made perfect. His healing power is magnified in our weakness, and His grace covers every area of our lives. No matter how deep the pain, the Savior's healing touch can reach us and restore us.

The Savior's healing is not just about the here and now—it is about eternity. When He heals our hearts, He is preparing us for the eternal life He has promised. Revelation 21:4 gives us a glimpse of this promise: "And God shall wipe away all tears from their eyes; and there shall be no more death, neither sorrow, nor crying, neither shall there be any more pain: for the former things are passed away." The healing and restoration we experience in this life are just a foretaste of the complete healing we will experience in eternity. In His presence, all of our pain and sorrow will be wiped away, and we will be made whole in every way. The Savior's reach into our broken hearts is not just about mending what is broken now, but about preparing us for the perfect joy and peace we will experience in His presence forever.

In the midst of our brokenness, it can be hard to see how healing and restoration are possible. The weight of the pain can feel overwhelming, and we may wonder if we will ever feel whole again. But the Savior's promise is sure: He is the healer of broken hearts, and He will restore us. In Matthew 11:28, Jesus invites us, "Come unto me, all ye that labour and are heavy laden, and I will give you rest." The Savior doesn't ask us to fix ourselves or to carry the burden of our pain alone. He invites us to come to Him, to lay our burdens at His feet, and to let Him do the work of healing in our hearts. His rest is not just physical rest, but rest for our souls—the deep peace that comes from knowing that we are loved, that we are forgiven, and that we are being made whole in Him.

In conclusion, the Savior reaches into broken hearts to bring healing and restoration, and His healing is complete, powerful, and available to all who come to Him. Whether our brokenness is caused by our own mistakes, the pain of loss, or the wounds inflicted by others, the Savior's love is enough to heal us. He binds up our wounds, He gives us a new heart, and He restores what has been broken. His healing touch brings peace, comfort, and hope, even in the darkest moments of our lives. The Savior's reach is infinite, and His desire is to see every heart healed and restored to the fullness of life in Him. No matter how broken we feel, no matter how deep the pain, the Savior is there, offering His healing and His love, and we can trust that He will complete the work He has begun in us, making us whole again in His perfect time.

Chapter 4 - The Savior reaches into the darkest places of sin to bring forgiveness.

The Savior reaches into the darkest places of sin to bring forgiveness, and there is no depth of sin, no level of guilt or shame that His grace cannot overcome. His love for us is so great that He pursues us even when we are at our lowest, when we feel the farthest from Him. In the darkest moments of our lives, when we have fallen into sin and feel unworthy of God's love, the Savior steps in with His boundless mercy and offers us a way out, a way back to Him. The Bible reminds us in Romans 5:8, "But God commendeth his love toward us, in that, while we were yet sinners, Christ died for us." This verse reveals the heart of the Savior's love—He didn't wait for us to clean ourselves up, to become worthy of His love, or to stop sinning before He acted. He came to us in the middle of our sin, in the midst of our rebellion, and laid down His life to offer us forgiveness. His sacrifice on the cross was the ultimate expression of His love, reaching into the darkest places of our hearts to cleanse us, to free us from the chains of sin, and to restore our relationship with God.

The darkness of sin can feel overwhelming. It weighs us down, fills us with guilt and shame, and makes us feel distant from God. But no matter how far we feel from Him, the Savior is always reaching out to us, offering forgiveness and a new beginning. In 1 John 1:9, we are given this incredible promise: "If we confess our sins, he is faithful and just to forgive us our sins, and to cleanse us from all unrighteousness." The Savior's forgiveness is not conditional—it is not based on how bad or frequent our sins are. It is based on His faithfulness and His justice. He doesn't hold our sins against us; instead, He wipes them away completely, cleansing us from all unrighteousness. When we confess our sins to Him, He doesn't condemn us—He forgives us. He doesn't leave us in the darkness of our sin, but He brings us into the light of His grace, washing away our guilt and making us new.

There are times when the darkness of sin feels so great that we think we are beyond forgiveness. We may believe that our sins are too big, too numerous, or too shameful for God to forgive. But the Bible reassures us that the Savior's reach is limitless. Isaiah 1:18 says, "Come now, and let us reason together, saith the LORD: though your sins be as scarlet, they shall be as white as snow; though they be red like crimson, they shall be as wool." No matter how deep the stain of our sin, the Savior's forgiveness can make us clean. The red stain of guilt that seems impossible to remove is no match for the power of His blood, shed for us on the cross. When the Savior reaches into the darkness of our sin, He doesn't just cover it up or ignore it—He completely washes it away, making us pure and spotless in His sight. His forgiveness is total and complete, transforming our lives and giving us a fresh start.

The Savior's reach into the darkest places of sin is motivated by His incredible love for us. He does not want us to remain trapped in sin, burdened by guilt or separated from God. His desire is for us to be free, to live in the fullness of His love and grace. In John 8:36, Jesus says, "If the Son therefore shall make you free, ye shall be free indeed." This is the freedom the Savior offers us—the freedom from the power of sin, the freedom from guilt, and the freedom to live in the light of His forgiveness. When we are trapped in the darkness of sin, it can feel like there is no way out. The enemy whispers lies to us, telling us that we are too far gone, that God could never forgive us, and that we will always be defined by our mistakes. But the Savior's truth is so much greater than the enemy's lies. His reach is greater than our sin, and His forgiveness is greater than our guilt. He breaks the chains that sin has placed on us, and He brings us into a life of freedom and grace.

Throughout the Bible, we see countless examples of the Savior reaching into the darkest places of sin to bring forgiveness. One of the most powerful stories is that of the prodigal son in Luke 15. The son had made terrible choices, squandered his inheritance, and found himself in a pit of despair and sin. He was in the darkest place of his life, far from his father, filled with guilt and shame. But when he decided to return home, even though he felt unworthy, his father ran to him, embraced him, and celebrated his return. This is the heart of the Savior—He doesn't wait for us to earn His forgiveness; He runs to meet us the moment we turn to Him. In Luke 15:24, the father says, "For this my son was dead, and is alive again; he was lost, and is found." This is what the Savior does for us—He brings us back to life, back from the deadness of sin, and into the joy of being found in Him. No matter how lost we feel, no matter how far we have wandered, the Savior is always ready to welcome us back with open arms, offering forgiveness and restoration.

Another powerful example of the Savior's reach into the darkest places of sin is His interaction with the woman caught in adultery in John 8. The religious leaders brought her to Jesus, expecting Him to condemn her, to punish her for her sin. But instead, Jesus offered her forgiveness. He said to her, "Neither do I condemn thee: go, and sin no more" (John 8:11). This is the heart of the Savior—He does not condemn us for our sins; He offers us forgiveness and the opportunity to live a new life. He reaches into the darkest places of our sin, not to shame us, but to free us. His forgiveness is not a license to continue in sin, but an invitation to walk in the light, to leave behind the darkness, and to live in the freedom He has given us. The woman's life was forever changed because the Savior reached into her darkest moment and offered her forgiveness instead of judgment. This is what He does for each of us—He offers us forgiveness when we deserve judgment, and He gives us grace when we deserve punishment.

The Savior's forgiveness is also a reflection of His incredible mercy. In Ephesians 2:4-5, we are reminded, "But God, who is rich in mercy, for his great love wherewith he loved us, even when we were dead in sins, hath quickened us together with Christ, (by grace ye are saved)." The Savior's mercy is what compels Him to reach into the darkest places of our sin and offer us life. We were spiritually dead in our sins, but because of His great love and mercy, He has made us alive in Him. His mercy is not something we can earn or deserve—it is a gift that flows from His heart of love. When we are weighed down by the guilt of our sins, the Savior's mercy lifts that burden from us. He does not treat us as our sins deserve, but instead, He offers us grace, forgiveness, and new life.

The Savior's reach into the darkest places of sin is also a demonstration of His victory over sin and death. Through His death and resurrection, He conquered the power of sin, making it possible for us to be forgiven and set free. In 1 Corinthians 15:57, we are told, "But thanks be to God, which giveth us the victory through our Lord Jesus Christ." The Savior's victory is our victory. We no longer have to live under the weight of sin because He has already won the battle for us. His forgiveness is not just a temporary fix—it is a permanent solution to the problem of sin. When He forgives us, He removes our sins from us as far as the east is from the west (Psalm 103:12). Our sins are completely and forever dealt with through the power of His blood, shed for us on the cross. This is the power of the Savior's reach—He not only forgives us, but He removes the stain of sin from our lives, giving us a new identity as children of God.

In conclusion, the Savior reaches into the darkest places of sin to bring forgiveness, and His forgiveness is greater than any sin we could ever commit. No matter how far we have fallen, no matter how deep the darkness of our sin, the Savior's reach is always enough. He offers us forgiveness, not based on our worthiness, but based on His love, His mercy, and His grace. His forgiveness washes away the guilt and shame that sin brings, and it gives us the freedom to live in the light of His love. The Savior's reach into our sin is a demonstration of His incredible love for us—a love that pursued us even when we were still sinners, a love that led Him to the cross, and a love that continues to offer us forgiveness every time we fall. The darkness of sin can never overcome the light of the Savior's grace, and His reach is infinite, always offering us a way out of the darkness and into the light of His forgiveness. No matter where we are or how far we feel from God, we can always turn to the Savior and receive the forgiveness He so freely offers.

Chapter 5 - The Savior reaches through the corridors of time to offer eternal life.

The Savior reaches through the corridors of time to offer eternal life, extending His love and grace from eternity past to eternity future. His gift of eternal life is not bound by time, culture, or human limitations; it is a timeless offer that He extends to everyone who believes. When we think of eternal life, it is not just life that goes on forever; it is the fullness of life, the life that is found only in the Savior, Jesus Christ. His reach spans across every generation, every nation, and every soul that has ever walked this earth, as He invites each one to receive the gift of eternal life. John 3:16 captures this promise perfectly: "For God so loved the world, that he gave his only begotten Son, that whosoever believeth in him should not perish, but have everlasting life." This verse reveals the depth of God's love and the incredible reach of the Savior's grace. He reaches through all of history, through every mistake, every sin, every rebellion, and still offers us life that never ends. Eternal life is not something we can earn, nor is it something we deserve—it is a free gift from the Savior, given through His sacrifice on the cross. His love for us is so great that He stepped into time, took on human flesh, and died for our sins, so that we might live with Him forever. This is the heart of the Savior—He desires that we spend eternity with Him, and He has made a way for that to happen through His death and resurrection.

The Savior's reach through the corridors of time is not just a future promise; it is a present reality. Eternal life begins the moment we put our faith in Jesus Christ. In John 17:3, Jesus says, "And this is life eternal, that they might know thee the only true God, and Jesus Christ, whom thou hast sent." Eternal life is not just about living forever—it is about knowing God, experiencing His love, His peace, and His presence in our lives right now. The Savior reaches into our present, offering us a relationship with Him that transcends time and circumstance. This relationship is what gives us hope in the midst of life's challenges, because we know that no matter what happens, we are secure in His hands for all eternity. The Savior's offer of eternal life is not something we have to wait for; it is something we can experience today, as we walk with Him and grow in our knowledge of Him.

The promise of eternal life is one that stretches back to the very beginning of time. From the moment sin entered the world, God had a plan to redeem humanity and restore us to eternal life with Him. In Genesis 3:15, we see the first glimpse of this plan, when God says to the serpent, "And I will put enmity between thee and the woman, and between thy seed and her seed; it shall bruise thy head, and thou shalt bruise his heel." This is the promise of the Savior, the one who would come to crush the power of sin and death and offer eternal life to all who believe in Him. Throughout the Old Testament, we see the unfolding of this plan, as God reaches through time, preparing the way for the coming of Jesus Christ, the Savior of the world. Every prophecy, every promise, every act of God in history points to the moment when the Savior would come, offering eternal life through His death and resurrection.

The Savior's reach is not limited by time or space. His offer of eternal life is for all people, in every generation, from the beginning of time until the end. 2 Peter 3:9 reminds us, "The Lord is not slack concerning his promise, as some men count slackness; but is longsuffering to us-ward, not willing that any should perish, but that all should come to repentance." The Savior's desire is that no one should be lost, that no one should miss out on the gift of eternal life. His patience with us, His willingness to wait, is a reflection of His great love. He reaches through time, giving each person the opportunity to come to Him, to repent, and to receive the life that He offers. The Savior's heart is for every person, in every place, in every era, to come to know Him and to live forever in His presence.

Eternal life is more than just a concept; it is the very reason the Savior came to earth. In John 10:10, Jesus says, "I am come that they might have life, and that they might have it more abundantly." The Savior didn't come just to give us a longer life—He came to give us a life that is full, abundant, and overflowing with His love and grace. This abundant life is the life we are invited into when we accept His offer of eternal life. It is a life that is not defined by the things of this world, but by the relationship we have with the Savior. The joy, peace, and purpose that come from knowing Him are just a taste of the eternal life we will experience fully when we are with Him in heaven. The Savior's reach into our lives is not just about getting us into heaven; it is about bringing heaven into our hearts right now.

When we think about the Savior reaching through time to offer eternal life, we cannot ignore the fact that this offer came at a great cost. Eternal life is a free gift to us, but it cost the Savior everything. Romans 6:23 tells us, "For the wages of sin is death; but the gift of God is eternal life through Jesus Christ our Lord." The death that we deserved because of our sin was taken by Jesus on the cross. He paid the price so that we could receive the gift of eternal life. This is the greatest act of love the world has ever known—that the Savior would give His life for us, so that we could live with Him forever. His reach into the corridors of time is marked by the cross, where He defeated death and made a way for us to have eternal life. His sacrifice was once for all, and through it, He secured our eternal future.

The Savior's offer of eternal life is not just about the quantity of life—it is about the quality of life. In Revelation 21:4, we are given a glimpse of what this eternal life will look like: "And God shall wipe away all tears from their eyes; and there shall be no more death, neither sorrow, nor crying, neither shall there be any more pain: for the former things are passed away." Eternal life is a life free from pain, suffering, and death. It is a life where we will be fully in the presence of God, experiencing His love and joy in ways we can only imagine right now. The Savior reaches through time to offer us this kind of life, not just in the future, but as a promise we can hold onto today. No matter what we face in this life, we can have hope because we know that eternal life with the Savior is waiting for us.

The Savior's reach through time also reminds us that eternity is not just something that begins when we die—it is something that is already unfolding. In Ecclesiastes 3:11, we are told, "He hath made every thing beautiful in his time: also he hath set the world in their heart, so that no man can find out the work that God maketh from the beginning to the end." God has placed eternity in our hearts, and the Savior invites us to live in the reality of eternity now. When we accept the Savior's offer of eternal life, we begin to live in the light of eternity. Our perspective changes, our priorities shift, and we begin to see life through the lens of eternity. The things that once seemed so important in this world begin to fade in comparison to the glory of eternal life with the Savior.

The Savior's reach through time to offer eternal life is a reminder that our lives are part of a much bigger story. We are not just here by accident, and our lives are not just a fleeting moment in history. We are part of God's eternal plan, a plan that has been unfolding since the beginning of time. Ephesians 1:4 tells us, "According as he hath chosen us in him before the foundation of the world, that we should be holy and without blame before him in love." The Savior chose us before the foundation of the world, and His offer of eternal life is part of His plan for us. We were created for eternity, and the Savior's reach into our lives is a reminder that we are loved, valued, and known by Him.

As we think about the Savior reaching through the corridors of time to offer eternal life, we are reminded that time itself will one day come to an end, but eternal life with the Savior will never end. In Revelation 22:13, Jesus says, "I am Alpha and Omega, the beginning and the end, the first and the last." The Savior is the beginning and the end of all things, and His offer of eternal life is an invitation to be with Him for all eternity. The time we have on this earth is limited, but the life we have in the Savior is eternal. His reach into our lives is an invitation to step out of the limitations of time and into the boundless joy of eternity with Him.

In conclusion, the Savior reaches through the corridors of time to offer eternal life, and His offer is one of love, grace, and endless joy. Eternal life is not just about living forever—it is about living in the fullness of God's presence, experiencing His love and grace every day. The Savior's reach is infinite, spanning across history, across cultures, across generations, and across every individual life. He invites each one of us to receive this gift of eternal life, not because we deserve it, but because of His incredible love for us. His reach is not limited by time, by our mistakes, or by our circumstances—He reaches out to us with open arms, offering us a life that will never end. The Savior's reach is a reminder that we are part of something so much bigger than ourselves, something that stretches beyond time and into eternity. Eternal life with the Savior is the greatest gift we could ever receive, and it is a gift that He offers to each one of us, today and forever.

Chapter 6 - The Savior reaches into our pain to bring comfort and peace.

The Savior reaches into our pain to bring comfort and peace, and His touch is like no other. In the darkest and most difficult moments of our lives, when the weight of sorrow, disappointment, and suffering feels unbearable, the Savior comes close, reaching into the depths of our hearts to bring the comfort that only He can give. He knows our pain intimately, and He is not distant or detached from it. He steps into our brokenness, our grief, and our hurt, wrapping us in His love and offering us peace that surpasses all understanding. In Matthew 11:28, Jesus invites us, saying, "Come unto me, all ye that labour and are heavy laden, and I will give you rest." This is the heart of the Savior—He sees the burdens we carry, the pain we try to hide, and He gently calls us to bring it all to Him. He doesn't demand that we fix ourselves or find our own way out of the darkness; instead, He offers us rest for our souls, peace for our troubled minds, and comfort for our aching hearts. His reach is tender and compassionate, knowing exactly what we need in the midst of our pain.

Pain is a universal experience, and at some point in life, we all face moments of heartache, loss, or struggle. Whether it's the loss of a loved one, a broken relationship, the disappointment of unmet dreams, or the crushing weight of anxiety and fear, pain can feel isolating, as if no one truly understands what we're going through. But the Savior does. Isaiah 53:3 describes Jesus as "a man of sorrows, and acquainted with grief." He knows what it means to suffer. He knows what it feels like to carry the weight of the world's pain, for He carried it all on the cross. The very One who created the universe also experienced the depths of human pain, and because of that, He is able to meet us in our suffering with empathy, grace, and healing. The Savior doesn't just offer superficial comfort—He enters into our pain with us, walking alongside us through the valleys of life, holding us up when we feel like we can't take another step.

When we are overwhelmed by pain, it can be hard to see a way out. The weight of sorrow can cloud our vision, making it feel as though peace and comfort are out of reach. But the Savior's promise to us is clear: He is our refuge and strength, a very present help in trouble (Psalm 46:1). His presence is our safe place, our shelter from the storms of life. He doesn't take away the reality of pain, but He gives us a place to rest, a place to find solace and security in His loving arms. When we run to Him, He surrounds us with His peace, a peace that calms the chaos in our hearts and minds, even when the circumstances around us remain difficult. Philippians 4:7 reminds us that "the peace of God, which passeth all understanding, shall keep your hearts and minds through Christ Jesus." This peace is not something we can manufacture on our own; it is a gift from the Savior, given to us as we trust Him with our pain, our fears, and our uncertainties.

The Savior's comfort is not like the temporary relief the world offers. The world may try to distract us from our pain with entertainment, busyness, or empty promises, but these things only offer fleeting moments of escape. The Savior, however, offers lasting comfort that goes deep into our souls. In John 14:27, Jesus says, "Peace I leave with you, my peace I give unto you: not as the world giveth, give I unto you. Let not your heart be troubled, neither let it be afraid." The peace that the Savior gives is not based on our circumstances; it is rooted in His presence with us. Even when the pain doesn't go away immediately, His peace remains, steady and sure, holding us up when we feel like we're falling apart. The Savior's peace is the anchor for our souls, keeping us grounded in His love and grace, no matter how strong the storms of life may be.

In moments of deep pain, we often cry out for answers, wanting to know why we are suffering or when the pain will end. But more than answers, the Savior gives us Himself. He doesn't always explain the reasons behind our suffering, but He promises to be with us through it. In Psalm 34:18, we are reminded, "The LORD is nigh unto them that are of a broken heart; and saveth such as be of a contrite spirit." The Savior draws near to us in our brokenness, and His nearness is the greatest comfort we could ever receive. When we feel abandoned, forgotten, or misunderstood, the Savior whispers to our hearts that we are not alone. He is with us, holding us close, wiping away our tears, and reminding us that He sees our pain and cares deeply about it.

The Savior's comfort is also a promise of healing. While we may not experience complete healing in this life, the Savior is always working to restore and renew our hearts. In Revelation 21:4, we are given a glimpse of the future promise: "And God shall wipe away all tears from their eyes; and there shall be no more death, neither sorrow, nor crying, neither shall there be any more pain: for the former things are passed away." The pain we experience now is temporary, but the comfort the Savior offers is eternal. He is preparing a place for us where there will be no more suffering, no more heartache, and no more tears. This promise gives us hope in the midst of our pain, reminding us that the Savior's comfort is not just for today, but for eternity.

In the here and now, the Savior comforts us by carrying our burdens with us. In 1 Peter 5:7, we are told, "Casting all your care upon him; for he careth for you." The Savior doesn't just stand by and watch us struggle; He invites us to cast our cares, our worries, our fears, and our pain onto Him, because He cares for us. He is not indifferent to our suffering—He cares deeply, and He is strong enough to carry the weight of our burdens. When we feel like we can't take another step, the Savior lifts the load off our shoulders and carries it for us. His strength becomes our strength, and His comfort becomes our source of peace.

The Savior's comfort is not just for our own healing—it is also meant to be shared with others. In 2 Corinthians 1:3-4, we read, "Blessed be God, even the Father of our Lord Jesus Christ, the Father of mercies, and the God of all comfort; who comforteth us in all our tribulation, that we may be able to comfort them which are in any trouble, by the comfort wherewith we ourselves are comforted of God." The comfort we receive from the Savior is meant to overflow into the lives of others. As we experience His healing and peace, we are able to extend that same comfort to those around us who are hurting. The Savior uses our own pain and the comfort we receive to make us instruments of His grace, helping others find hope and peace in Him.

The Savior's reach into our pain is an act of love. He doesn't turn away from our suffering; He enters into it with us, just as He entered into the suffering of the world when He took on human flesh and died on the cross. Isaiah 53:4 reminds us, "Surely he hath borne our griefs, and carried our sorrows."

The Savior has already carried the full weight of our pain, and because of His sacrifice, we can trust that He understands our suffering and is with us in the midst of it. He is not a distant, detached Savior—He is Immanuel, God with us, the One who walks with us through every trial, every heartache, and every moment of pain.

In the end, the Savior's comfort and peace are a reflection of His unchanging character. He is the Prince of Peace (Isaiah 9:6), and His peace is not dependent on our circumstances, but on His faithfulness. Even when everything around us is falling apart, the Savior remains the same—steady, faithful, and full of love. His peace is not something we have to earn or strive for; it is a gift that He freely gives to those who come to Him in their pain. When we feel like we are drowning in sorrow, the Savior is there, reaching out His hand to lift us up, to calm the storm, and to bring us into His perfect peace.

In conclusion, the Savior reaches into our pain to bring comfort and peace, and His reach is always enough. No matter how deep the pain, no matter how overwhelming the sorrow, the Savior's comfort is greater. He is near to the brokenhearted, He carries our burdens, and He offers us a peace that the world cannot give. His love for us is unshakable, and His presence is our refuge in times of trouble. As we cast our cares on Him, we find rest for our souls, knowing that He cares for us deeply and will never leave us. The Savior's comfort is a promise of healing, both now and in eternity, and His peace is a gift that holds us steady in the midst of life's storms. We can trust the Savior to meet us in our pain, to walk with us through it, and to bring us the peace that only He can give.

Chapter 7 - The Savior reaches across the divide of death to offer resurrection and life.

The Savior reaches across the divide of death to offer resurrection and life, and His victory over death is the foundation of our hope. Death is something that every human being must face, and for many, it brings fear and uncertainty. It feels final, like an unbreakable wall that separates us from life, from joy, and from everything we have ever known. But the Savior, Jesus Christ, broke through that wall. He conquered death once and for all, and in doing so, He opened the way for us to experience eternal life. His resurrection is the most powerful demonstration of His authority over life and death, and because He lives, we too can have the promise of life beyond the grave. Jesus Himself declared in John 11:25-26, "I am the resurrection, and the life: he that believeth in me, though he were dead, yet shall he live: and whosoever liveth and believeth in me shall never die." This promise from the Savior is not just for some distant future—it is for us now. Death does not have the final word. The Savior does. He has reached across the chasm that death creates and offers us the gift of eternal life through His own death and resurrection.

In the face of death, we often feel powerless. The loss of a loved one, the reality of our own mortality, the pain and sorrow that death brings—these are some of the most difficult experiences we endure. But the Savior's reach extends into the deepest darkness, even the darkness of death, to bring light and hope. In John 14:19, Jesus offers this reassurance: "Because I live, ye shall live also." His resurrection is the guarantee that death is not the end for those who believe in Him. While we may still experience physical death, it is no longer something to fear, because the Savior has transformed it into a passageway to eternal life. For the believer, death is not a destination but a doorway into the presence of God, where there is no more pain, no more sorrow, and no more separation. Revelation 21:4 gives us this beautiful promise of what lies beyond death: "And

God shall wipe away all tears from their eyes; and there shall be no more death, neither sorrow, nor crying, neither shall there be any more pain: for the former things are passed away."

The Savior's reach across the divide of death is made possible because of His own death on the cross and His glorious resurrection three days later. Jesus willingly laid down His life for us, taking the punishment for our sins, so that we might be forgiven and have the opportunity to experience eternal life. Romans 6:23 tells us, "For the wages of sin is death; but the gift of God is eternal life through Jesus Christ our Lord." Because of sin, death entered the world, and it became the fate of every human being. But the Savior, in His infinite love and mercy, took our place. He bore the full weight of death and sin so that we would not have to. His resurrection was the ultimate victory over death, proving that He has the power to give life to all who believe in Him. When the stone was rolled away from the tomb, and Jesus walked out alive, He declared once and for all that death had been defeated.

This victory over death is not something we can achieve on our own. It is a gift, freely given by the Savior to all who place their faith in Him. In 1 Corinthians 15:55-57, Paul writes, "O death, where is thy sting? O grave, where is thy victory? The sting of death is sin; and the strength of sin is the law. But thanks be to God, which giveth us the victory through our Lord Jesus Christ." The sting of death, the pain that it causes, is removed because of what the Savior has done. The grave no longer has victory over us, because we have been given the victory through Jesus Christ. This is the hope that we cling to, the hope that sustains us even in the face of death. Because the Savior has reached across the divide of death, we can look forward to resurrection and eternal life, knowing that nothing—not even death—can separate us from His love.

The promise of resurrection and life is not just for the future; it changes how we live today. Knowing that the Savior has overcome death gives us courage and peace in the midst of life's trials. In 1 Thessalonians 4:13-14, Paul encourages believers with these words: "But I would not have you to be ignorant, brethren, concerning them which are asleep, that ye sorrow not, even as others which have no hope. For if we believe that Jesus died and rose again, even so them also which sleep in Jesus will God bring with him." When we lose someone we love, it is natural to grieve, but as believers, we do not grieve without hope. We know that those who have died in Christ will be raised to life again, and we will be reunited with them in the presence of the Savior. The separation that death brings is only temporary, because the Savior has promised to bring us all into His eternal kingdom, where we will live forever with Him.

The Savior's reach across the divide of death also transforms our understanding of what it means to die. For those who are in Christ, death is not something to fear, but something to look forward to, because it brings us into the fullness of life with God. In Philippians 1:21, Paul expresses this perspective: "For to me to live is Christ, and to die is gain." While we live on this earth, we have the opportunity to serve the Savior and grow in our relationship with Him. But when we die, we gain the indescribable joy of being with Him for all eternity. Death, for the believer, is not a loss, but a gain. It is the moment when we leave behind the brokenness of this world and enter into the perfect, unending life that the Savior has prepared for us.

The reality of resurrection and eternal life gives us hope not only for the future, but for the present. Because we know that death has been defeated, we can live with confidence and purpose. In John 10:10, Jesus says, "I am come that they might have life, and that they might have it more abundantly." The Savior offers us abundant life—not just in eternity, but here and now. This abundant life is not defined by the absence of trouble or hardship, but by the presence of the Savior with us in every moment. It is a life filled with His love, His peace, and His joy, knowing that no matter what we face, even death itself, we are secure in His hands. The Savior's reach across the divide of death gives us the assurance that nothing can separate us from His love. Romans 8:38-39 declares, "For I am persuaded, that neither death, nor life, nor angels, nor principalities, nor powers, nor things present, nor things to come, nor height, nor depth, nor any other creature, shall be able to separate us from the love of God, which is in Christ Jesus our Lord."

Because the Savior has reached across the divide of death, we can face the future with hope and peace. We know that our lives are not confined to the few years we spend on this earth, but that we have an eternity waiting for us in the presence of God. This hope gives us strength to endure the difficulties of life, knowing that they are only temporary, and that the joy of eternal life with the Savior far outweighs any suffering we experience now. In 2 Corinthians 4:17, Paul writes, "For our light affliction, which is but for a moment, worketh for us a far more exceeding and eternal weight of glory." The pain, the loss, and the trials of this life are real, but they are not the end of the story. The Savior's promise of resurrection and life gives us the perspective we need to persevere, trusting that the glory that awaits us in eternity far surpasses anything we could imagine.

The Savior's reach across the divide of death is also a call to faith. He offers the gift of eternal life, but we must choose to accept it. In John 5:24, Jesus says, "Verily, verily, I say unto you, He that heareth my word, and believeth on him that sent me, hath everlasting life, and shall not come into condemnation; but is passed from death unto life." The moment we place our faith in the Savior, we pass from death to life. We no longer have to fear judgment or condemnation, because the Savior has taken that upon Himself. His death and resurrection have made it possible for us to be forgiven, to be made new, and to receive the gift of eternal life. This is the greatest gift we could ever receive, and it is available to all who believe in Him.

In conclusion, the Savior reaches across the divide of death to offer resurrection and life, and His victory over death is the foundation of our hope. Through His death and resurrection, He has broken the power of sin and death, and He offers us the gift of eternal life. Death is no longer something to fear, because the Savior has transformed it into a doorway to eternal life with Him. His reach extends beyond the grave, offering us the promise of resurrection, the joy of eternal life, and the peace that comes from knowing that nothing—not even death—can separate us from His love. The Savior's reach across the divide of death is a demonstration of His incredible love for us, a love that pursued us even to the point of death on a cross, so that we might live forever with Him. Because He lives, we too can live, both now and for all eternity. This is the hope that sustains us, the hope that gives us peace, and the

hope that assures us that death has been defeated and life has won. The Savior's reach is infinite, and His offer of resurrection and life is available to all who place their faith in Him.

Chapter 8 - The Savior reaches into the minds filled with doubt to bring truth and clarity.

The Savior reaches into minds filled with doubt to bring truth and clarity, and there is no confusion, uncertainty, or fear that His light cannot dispel. Doubt is something we all face at times. Whether it's doubt about ourselves, doubt about our future, or even doubt about God, it can cloud our minds, leaving us feeling lost and unsure. But the Savior, in His infinite wisdom and love, sees our struggles and steps into our confusion, offering us the truth that sets us free. His reach is not hindered by our questions or hesitations; He lovingly guides us from the darkness of doubt into the clarity of His truth. In James 1:5, we are given this incredible promise: "If any of you lack wisdom, let him ask of God, that giveth to all men liberally, and upbraideth not; and it shall be given him." The Savior does not turn us away when we come to Him with our doubts. Instead, He invites us to seek His wisdom, to ask Him for understanding, and to trust that He will generously provide the answers we need. His truth is not hidden or distant—it is available to all who come to Him with open hearts, ready to listen and receive.

Doubt can feel like a heavy burden, weighing us down and making it difficult to move forward. It can paralyze us, causing us to second-guess everything we believe, everything we know to be true. But the Savior's truth is a light that cuts through the fog of doubt, bringing clarity and direction. In John 8:32, Jesus says, "And ye shall know the truth, and the truth shall make you free." The truth that the Savior offers is not just an intellectual understanding; it is a truth that sets us free from the chains of doubt, fear, and uncertainty. It is the truth of who He is—our Savior, our Redeemer, the One who never changes, even when everything around us does. His truth is solid and unshakable, a firm foundation we can stand on when doubt tries to pull us under. No matter how deep our doubts may go, the Savior's truth goes deeper, reaching into the very core of our hearts and minds, anchoring us in His love and faithfulness.

The Savior understands our doubts because He walked this earth as we do. He knows what it means to face uncertainty, to wrestle with questions, and to seek the will of the Father. In the Garden of Gethsemane, Jesus Himself experienced a moment of deep anguish and questioning, as He prayed, "O my Father, if it be possible, let this cup pass from me: nevertheless not as I will, but as thou wilt" (Matthew 26:39). In that moment, we see that even the Savior understands what it means to struggle with doubt and fear. But He also shows us the way through it—by trusting in the Father's will, by surrendering our doubts to God, and by leaning on His truth. The Savior doesn't condemn us for our doubts; instead, He meets us in them, just as He met the disciple Thomas after His resurrection. Thomas, filled with doubt, said he would not believe unless he could see the wounds in Jesus' hands and side for himself. And Jesus, in His compassion, appeared to Thomas and said, "Reach hither thy finger, and behold my hands; and reach hither thy hand, and thrust it into my side: and be not faithless, but believing" (John 20:27). The Savior didn't shame Thomas for his doubts—He invited him to come closer, to see and believe. This is how the Savior reaches into our minds filled with doubt—He doesn't push us away; He invites us to draw near, to ask our questions, and to find the answers in Him.

When we are filled with doubt, it can feel as though we are walking in darkness, unsure of where to go or what to believe. But the Savior is the light of the world, and His light shines in the darkness, bringing clarity to our minds and peace to our hearts. In John 8:12, Jesus says, "I am the light of the world: he that followeth me shall not walk in darkness, but shall have the light of life." The light that the Savior offers is not just a flicker of hope—it is the brilliant, unchanging light of His truth, guiding us out of the darkness of doubt and into the light of His presence. When we follow Him, we no longer have to stumble through life, uncertain and afraid. His light illuminates our path, showing us the way forward, and His truth gives us the confidence to trust Him, even when we don't have all the answers.

One of the most powerful ways the Savior reaches into our doubts is through His Word. The Bible is filled with the truth that we need to combat the lies and confusion that doubt brings. In Psalm 119:105, we read, "Thy word is a lamp unto my feet, and a light unto my path." When we are struggling with doubt, the Savior's Word is the light that shows us the way. It is filled with promises of His faithfulness, His love, and His unchanging nature. When everything else feels uncertain, we can turn to His Word and be reminded of what is true. The Savior uses Scripture to speak to our hearts, to reassure us of His presence, and to fill us with the wisdom and understanding we need. In a world that is constantly shifting and changing, the Savior's Word remains the same, and it is through His Word that He brings clarity to our minds.

Doubt often creeps in when we are faced with difficult circumstances or when life doesn't go the way we expected. It's in these moments that we begin to question God's plan, His goodness, or His presence in our lives. But the Savior reaches into these moments of doubt with the truth that He is always with us, even when we can't see it. In Isaiah 41:10, God promises, "Fear thou not; for I am with thee: be not dismayed; for I am thy God: I will strengthen thee; yea, I will help thee; yea, I will uphold thee with the right hand of my righteousness." This is the truth that the Savior speaks into our doubt—He is with us. He will never leave us or forsake us, and no matter how overwhelming our doubts may feel, His presence is constant and unchanging. When we are tempted to doubt His goodness or His faithfulness, the Savior reminds us of His promises, and His promises are always true.

Another powerful example of the Savior reaching into doubt can be seen in the story of Peter walking on the water. In Matthew 14, Peter stepped out of the boat in faith, walking toward Jesus on the water. But when he saw the wind and the waves, he became afraid and began to sink. In that moment of doubt and fear, Peter cried out, "Lord, save me!" And immediately, Jesus reached out His hand and caught him, saying, "O thou of little faith, wherefore didst thou doubt?" (Matthew 14:30-31). The Savior didn't let Peter drown in his doubt—He reached out and saved him. And then, He gently reminded Peter of the importance of keeping his eyes on Him, rather than on the storm. This is what the Savior does for us. When we are sinking in doubt, He reaches out His hand, lifts us up, and reminds us to focus on Him. The storms of life may be fierce, but the Savior is stronger. His truth is greater than any doubt we face, and when we keep our eyes on Him, we find the clarity and peace we need to keep moving forward.

The Savior's reach into our doubt is not just about answering our questions—it's about building our faith. Doubt is not the enemy of faith;

rather, it is an opportunity for our faith to grow deeper as we seek the truth. In Mark 9:24, we see the cry of a father who was struggling with doubt as he asked Jesus to heal his son. He said, "Lord, I believe; help thou mine unbelief." This simple yet powerful prayer is one that we can all relate to. Even in our belief, there are moments of doubt, moments when we need the Savior to strengthen our faith. And the Savior, in His grace, does just that. He helps us in our unbelief, guiding us through our doubts and bringing us to a place of deeper trust in Him.

Ultimately, the Savior reaches into our doubt to remind us of who He is. He is the way, the truth, and the life (John 14:6), and in Him, we find all the answers we need. Our doubts may cause us to question, but the Savior's truth remains unshakable. He is the solid rock on which we stand, and when we build our lives on His truth, we are able to withstand the storms of doubt that come our way. In Matthew 7:24-25, Jesus gives this promise: "Therefore whosoever heareth these sayings of mine, and doeth them, I will liken him unto a wise man, which built his house upon a rock: and the rain descended, and the floods came, and the winds blew, and beat upon that house; and it fell not: for it was founded upon a rock." The Savior is that rock, the unchanging truth that holds us steady when doubt threatens to shake us. When we build our lives on His truth, we are secure, no matter what comes our way.

In conclusion, the Savior reaches into minds filled with doubt to bring truth and clarity, and His truth is the light that guides us out of the darkness. He meets us in our doubts with compassion, not condemnation, and He invites us to come closer, to ask our questions, and to find the answers in Him. His Word is a lamp unto our feet, showing us the way when we feel lost and confused. His promises are the foundation we can stand on, even when everything else feels uncertain. The Savior's truth sets us free from the chains of doubt, giving us the peace and clarity we need to trust Him, even in the midst of life's challenges. No matter how deep our doubts may go, the Savior's reach is deeper. He is the way, the truth, and the life, and in Him, we find all the answers we need. His love for us is unshakable, and His truth is unchanging, offering us the clarity and confidence we need to walk in faith, even when we don't have all the answers. The Savior's reach into our doubt is a gift of grace, and as we lean into His truth, we are reminded that we are never alone—He is with us, guiding us, and giving us the clarity we need to trust Him fully.

Chapter 9 - The Savior reaches into every age, from childhood to old age, to extend grace.

The Savior reaches into every age, from childhood to old age, to extend grace, and His love knows no limits of time or age. From the moment a child takes their first breath until the last moments of life, the Savior's grace is constantly extended, always available to meet us right where we are. His grace is not reserved for the young or the old; it is for all people, at every stage of life, regardless of the circumstances we face. He cares for us deeply from the beginning to the end, and His hand is stretched out to guide, forgive, heal, and sustain us through every season of our lives. Psalm 71:17-18 beautifully reflects this truth: "O God, thou hast taught me from my youth: and hitherto have I declared thy wondrous works. Now also when I am old and grayheaded, O God, forsake me not." The Savior's grace is a constant companion, whether we are young and just learning about Him or we are old and have walked many years in His care. His love remains steady, His grace abundant, and His presence with us through it all.

In childhood, the Savior's grace is like a tender embrace, filled with compassion, care, and guidance. He calls children to come to Him, knowing that their hearts are pure and open to His love. Jesus made it clear how much He treasures children when He said, "Suffer little children to come unto me, and forbid them not: for of such is the kingdom of God" (Luke 18:16). The Savior's grace toward children is full of gentleness. He sees the innocence and vulnerability of young hearts, and He longs to fill them with His love and protection. Children may be small, but their faith is often large, and the Savior delights in welcoming them into His arms. His grace is a shelter for children, teaching them, nurturing them, and offering them a foundation of love that will guide them through the rest of their lives. Even when children are too young to fully understand who the Savior is, His grace is already at work in their lives, drawing them close to His heart and protecting them from the dangers of the world.

As children grow into adolescence, the Savior's grace continues to reach them, offering wisdom, understanding, and direction during a time of life that is often filled with confusion and change. Teenagers may wrestle with questions about their identity, their purpose, and their place in the world, but the Savior is always there, ready to offer the clarity and truth they need. James 1:5 reminds us, "If any of you lack wisdom, let him ask of God, that giveth to all men liberally, and upbraideth not; and it shall be given him." For young people who are navigating the challenges of growing up, the Savior's grace is like a compass, guiding them in the right direction, keeping them on the path of righteousness, and helping them make wise decisions that honor Him. His grace is patient, knowing that the journey of growing up is not easy. He gently leads teenagers through their doubts and struggles, offering them the assurance that they are deeply loved and valued by Him, no matter what.

As we enter adulthood, the Savior's grace takes on new dimensions, reaching us in the midst of the responsibilities, pressures, and challenges that life brings. Adulthood is a season of life where many are busy building careers, raising families, and making decisions that affect their future. It can be overwhelming at times, and many adults feel the weight of stress, worry, and exhaustion. But the Savior's grace is more than enough to meet the needs of adults who are carrying heavy burdens. In Matthew 11:28-30, Jesus offers this invitation: "Come unto me, all ye that labour and are heavy laden, and I will give you rest. Take my yoke upon you, and learn of me; for I am meek and lowly in heart: and ye shall find rest unto your souls. For my yoke is easy, and my burden is light." The Savior understands the pressures of adulthood, and His grace provides the strength, peace, and rest that adults so desperately need. His grace helps us to navigate the complexities of life, reminding us that we are not alone and that we can trust Him with every aspect of our lives.

For those in middle age, the Savior's grace reaches into the heart of life's transitions, offering stability and hope in times of change. Middle age is often a season where people reflect on their past and begin to look ahead to the future with new perspectives. It is a time when many face changes in their families, careers, and personal lives, and these changes can bring a mix of emotions—joy, uncertainty, and sometimes grief. But the Savior's grace is steadfast, anchoring us in His unchanging love. Isaiah 46:4 offers a comforting promise: "And even to your old age I am he; and even to hoar hairs will I carry you: I have made, and I will bear; even I will carry, and will deliver you." The Savior carries us through every stage of life, and in middle age, His grace is a source of strength, helping us to embrace the changes we face with confidence and faith. He walks with us through the highs and lows, offering wisdom for the road ahead and peace for the uncertainties we may feel.

As we enter the later years of life, the Savior's grace becomes a deep well of comfort, peace, and assurance. For the elderly, life often looks different than it once did. The pace may slow, physical abilities may decline, and there may be a sense of loss as friends and loved ones pass away or as the roles they once held change. But the Savior's grace never diminishes; in fact, it becomes even more precious in these later years. Psalm 92:14 speaks to the beauty of growing old in the Lord: "They shall still bring forth fruit in old age; they shall be fat and flourishing." Even in old age, the Savior's grace continues to bear fruit in our lives. He is not finished with us, no matter how old we are. His grace enables the elderly to continue serving Him, loving others, and living a life full of purpose. The Savior's presence is a source of comfort for those who may feel lonely or forgotten, and His grace is a reminder that their value in His eyes never fades. He is the constant companion for the elderly, walking with them through every season of life, and preparing them for the eternal life that awaits them with Him.

The Savior's grace extends not only to individuals at different stages of life but also to families as a whole. He is the source of grace that binds families together through the generations. Parents pass down the faith to their children, teaching them about the Savior's love and grace, and as children grow up, they carry that legacy of grace with them into adulthood. Proverbs 22:6 reminds us, "Train up a child in the way he should go: and when he is old, he will not depart from it." The Savior's grace flows through the generations, from parents to children to grandchildren, weaving His love and truth into the fabric of family life. He is the glue that holds families together, offering grace to forgive, to heal, and to strengthen relationships at every stage of life.

For those who may feel they have wasted years of their lives or have come to the Savior later in life, His grace is still there, reaching out to redeem the time. It doesn't matter how old we are or how much time has passed—the Savior's grace is always enough to cover our past and give us a new future. In Joel 2:25, God promises, "And I will restore to you the years that the locust hath eaten." The Savior can restore the years that we feel we have lost, whether through mistakes, sin, or circumstances beyond our control. His grace is redemptive, and He can use every part of our lives, no matter how broken or wasted we may feel, for His glory. The Savior's reach knows no limits, and His grace is always extended, even to those who come to Him later in life.

The Savior's grace is also a constant source of strength for those facing the end of life. As we approach the final years or months of our earthly journey, the Savior's grace is a comforting presence, assuring us that we do not walk this path alone. Psalm 23:4 offers this promise: "Yea, though I walk through the valley of the shadow of death, I will fear no evil: for thou art with me; thy rod and thy staff they comfort me." The Savior's grace is with us, even in the shadow of death. He leads us through it, not leaving us to face it in fear but bringing us into His eternal presence. His grace gives us peace as we look toward eternity, knowing that we will soon be with Him forever. For the believer, death is not the end—it is the beginning of eternal life with the Savior, where His grace will continue to abound for all eternity.

In conclusion, the Savior reaches into every age, from childhood to old age, to extend grace, and His grace is sufficient for every season of life. Whether we are children learning about His love for the first time, teenagers navigating the challenges of growing up, adults carrying the burdens of life, or elderly individuals reflecting on the years gone by, the Savior's grace is always there, always enough. He walks with us through every stage of life, offering us His love, His wisdom, His strength, and His peace. His grace is a constant source of hope, reminding us that we are never alone, no matter how old we are or what we are facing. From the first breath to the last, the Savior's grace is a gift that sustains us, carries us, and leads us into the fullness of life that He has prepared for us. The Savior's reach is infinite, and His grace extends to all who will receive it, offering us the promise of His presence and the assurance of His love through every moment of our lives.

Chapter 10 - The Savior reaches into the hardest hearts to soften them with love.

The Savior reaches into the hardest hearts to soften them with love, and His love is more powerful than any barrier, bitterness, or resistance that a heart may hold. No heart is too hard for Him to touch, no soul too far gone for His grace to reach. Even when people have turned away from Him, built walls around their hearts, or become consumed by anger, pain, or pride, the Savior's love never stops pursuing them. His love is relentless, patient, and filled with compassion. Ezekiel 36:26 gives us a beautiful promise of what the Savior can do in even the hardest heart: "A new heart also will I give you, and a new spirit will I put within you: and I will take away the stony heart out of your flesh, and I will give you an heart of flesh." The Savior does not just chip away at the hardness—He completely transforms the heart. He takes what was once cold and unfeeling, and He replaces it with a heart that is tender, responsive, and alive to His love. His love melts the hardest heart, breaking down the walls that have been built over time and allowing His grace to pour in, bringing healing, forgiveness, and renewal.

Hard hearts often develop over time, as a result of hurt, disappointment, betrayal, or fear. Life's challenges can cause people to become guarded, closing themselves off to others and to God in an effort to protect themselves from further pain. But the Savior sees beyond the hardness. He sees the pain that lies beneath the surface, and His heart is moved with compassion. In Matthew 11:28, Jesus invites all who are burdened and weary to come to Him, saying, "Come unto me, all ye that labour and are heavy laden, and I will give you rest." The hardness of heart often comes from carrying burdens for too long, from holding onto unforgiveness, or from the scars left by life's wounds. The Savior invites us to lay those burdens down, to surrender the hardness that has built up, and to allow His love to bring rest and peace to our souls. His love is the balm that heals the deepest wounds, and His grace is the key that unlocks the hardest heart, freeing us to experience His joy and peace once again.

The Bible gives us many examples of how the Savior's love softens even the hardest hearts. One of the most powerful stories of transformation is that of Saul, who later became known as the Apostle Paul. Saul was a man with a hard heart, filled with hatred and violence toward Christians. He actively persecuted the early church, imprisoning believers and approving of their deaths. Yet, even in the midst of his rebellion, the Savior's love reached out to Saul. In Acts 9, we see how Jesus met Saul on the road to Damascus, shining a light so bright that it blinded him and caused him to fall to the ground. Jesus spoke to him, saying, "Saul, Saul, why persecutest thou me?" (Acts 9:4). This moment was the turning point for Saul. The love of the Savior pierced through the hardness of his heart, and Saul was transformed into one of the greatest missionaries of the early church. The same man who once hated Christians became a man who loved them, spreading the message of Jesus' love and grace to the world. This story reminds us that no heart is too hard for the Savior's love to reach. His love can transform even the most hardened soul, turning them into a vessel of His grace.

Another example of the Savior's love reaching a hard heart is the story of Zacchaeus, a tax collector who was despised by his fellow Jews for his greed and dishonesty. Zacchaeus had built his life around selfishness and deceit, taking more than he was entitled to and living in a way that hurt others. But when Jesus came to Jericho and saw Zacchaeus in the tree, He called out to him and said, "Zacchaeus, make haste, and come down; for to day I must abide at thy house" (Luke 19:5). The Savior didn't reject Zacchaeus for his past or condemn him for his sins—He reached out to him with love, offering him forgiveness and a new beginning. Zacchaeus' heart was softened by the Savior's love, and in response, he repented of his wrongdoing and promised to make restitution to those he had wronged. The love of the Savior transformed Zacchaeus from a man consumed by greed into a man filled with generosity and grace. This is what the Savior's love does—it changes hearts, breaking down the walls of selfishness and sin and replacing them with a heart that is filled with love for God and others.

The Savior's love is also evident in the way He reaches out to those who have been hardened by sin and shame. The woman caught in adultery, in John 8, is a powerful example of how the Savior's love brings restoration to those whose hearts have been hardened by guilt and condemnation. When the religious leaders brought the woman to Jesus, accusing her of sin and demanding that she be punished, Jesus responded not with judgment but with love and mercy. He said to her, "Neither do I condemn thee: go, and sin no more" (John 8:11). The Savior's love softened her heart, not through harsh words or condemnation, but through grace and forgiveness. In that moment, the hardness of her heart melted away as she encountered the unconditional love of the Savior. His love set her free from the shame of her past and gave her the hope of a new life.

The Savior's love is relentless in its pursuit of those with hard hearts. Even when people have turned away from God, rejecting Him or running in the opposite direction, the Savior's love continues to follow them. The parable of the prodigal son, found in Luke 15, illustrates this beautifully. The younger son took his inheritance and left home, wasting it on wild living and eventually finding himself in a pit of despair. His heart had become hard, filled with pride and rebellion, but even in the far country, the love of his father—representing the love of the Savior—was waiting for him. When the son finally decided to return home, his father saw him from a distance and ran to meet him, embracing him and celebrating his return. The father's love softened the son's heart, leading him to repentance and reconciliation. This is how the Savior reaches out to us when we've wandered far from Him. His love never stops seeking us, never stops calling us back to Him, and when we finally turn toward Him, He runs to meet us with open arms, ready to forgive and restore.

The Savior's love is not only for those who have turned away—it is also for those who have been hardened by life's trials and suffering. Pain, disappointment, and loss can cause people to close off their hearts, becoming numb to the love of God and others. But even in these moments, the Savior's love is powerful enough to break through the hardness. In Psalm 147:3, we are reminded, "He healeth the broken in heart, and bindeth up their wounds." The Savior doesn't just see the hard exterior—He sees the brokenness underneath, and He tenderly brings healing to those who have been wounded by life's difficulties. His love is a balm that softens even the most calloused heart, bringing comfort, peace, and hope to those who feel like their hearts are too damaged to be healed. The Savior reaches into our pain with His love, gently softening our hearts and reminding us that we are never beyond His reach.

The Savior's love is also transformative for those whose hearts have been hardened by pride and self-righteousness. In the story of the Pharisee and the tax collector in Luke 18, we see how the Savior values humility over pride. The Pharisee prayed with arrogance, thanking God that he was not like other people, while the tax collector stood at a distance, humbly asking for God's mercy. Jesus said that it was the tax collector, not the Pharisee, who went home justified before God. "For every one that exalteth himself shall be abased; and he that humbleth himself shall be exalted" (Luke 18:14). The Savior's love reaches out to those who are filled with pride, offering them the opportunity to humble themselves and receive His grace. His love softens the heart of pride, replacing it with a heart of humility and gratitude.

In conclusion, the Savior reaches into the hardest hearts to soften them with love, and His love is powerful enough to break through any barrier. Whether it is a heart hardened by sin, pain, pride, or fear, the Savior's love is relentless in its pursuit, offering grace, forgiveness, and transformation. His love is not harsh or condemning—it is tender, compassionate, and full of mercy. He takes hearts that have become like stone and transforms them into hearts of flesh, alive and responsive to His love. The Savior's love has the power to melt the coldest heart, bringing healing and renewal to those who have been hardened by life's struggles. No heart is too hard for the Savior to reach, and His love never gives up on us. He is always reaching out, always inviting us to come to Him, to lay down our burdens, and to receive the fullness of His love and grace. The Savior's love is the greatest force in the world, and it is available to every heart, no matter how hard or broken it may be. As we open our hearts to Him, we will experience the transforming power of His love, and our hearts will be forever softened and renewed by His grace.

Chapter 11 - The Savior reaches into families to restore unity and love.

The Savior reaches into families to restore unity and love, mending the brokenness, healing the wounds, and bringing reconciliation where there has been division. In a world where families are often torn apart by conflict, misunderstandings, and pain, the Savior's love and grace offer the hope of restoration. His desire is for families to experience the fullness of His love, to live in harmony and peace, and to reflect the love that He has for us in their relationships with one another. From the very beginning, the family was designed by God to be a place of love, support, and connection. Yet, sin has caused fractures in families throughout history, leading to heartache, separation, and broken relationships. But the Savior steps into these broken places with His healing power, offering forgiveness, grace, and the ability to rebuild what has been lost. In Malachi 4:6, we see the promise of the Savior's work in restoring families: "And he shall turn the heart of the fathers to the children, and the heart of the children to their fathers." This is what the Savior does—He turns hearts back toward one another, softening them with His love, and bringing families back together.

Families face many challenges that can lead to division: arguments, misunderstandings, generational conflicts, and even betrayal. But the Savior's reach is not limited by the depth of the hurt or the length of time that families have been divided. His love is greater than any conflict, and His grace is stronger than any division. In Ephesians 4:31-32, the Bible urges us to "Let all bitterness, and wrath, and anger, and clamour, and evil speaking, be put away from you, with all malice: And be ye kind one to another, tenderhearted, forgiving one another, even as God for Christ's sake hath forgiven you." The Savior helps families to put away bitterness and anger, replacing it with kindness, tenderheartedness, and forgiveness. He enables us to forgive one another, even when it seems impossible, because He has first forgiven us. His grace flows into our hearts, giving us the strength to extend grace to those who have hurt us, and bringing healing where there has been deep pain.

The story of Joseph in the Bible is a powerful example of how the Savior's reach can restore unity and love within a family. Joseph's brothers betrayed him, selling him into slavery out of jealousy and hatred. For years, Joseph suffered as a result of their actions, but through it all, God's hand was at work. When Joseph eventually rose to power in Egypt, he was given the opportunity to confront his brothers. Instead of seeking revenge or holding onto the bitterness of the past, Joseph extended forgiveness to his brothers, saying, "But as for you, ye thought evil against me; but God meant it unto good" (Genesis 50:20). The Savior's grace had softened Joseph's heart, enabling him to forgive and to see God's greater purpose in the midst of the pain. As a result, Joseph's family was reunited, and the bonds of love were restored. This story reminds us that no matter how deep the wounds within a family, the Savior's love has the power to bring healing and reconciliation. He can take even the most broken situations and turn them into something beautiful, using the pain to strengthen the family and draw them closer to one another and to Him.

The Savior's work in restoring families is not just about healing past wounds—it's also about building a foundation of love and unity for the future. He teaches us how to love one another as He has loved us, with a love that is patient, kind, and selfless. In 1 Corinthians 13:4-7, we are given a picture of what love looks like: "Charity suffereth long, and is kind; charity envieth not; charity vaunteth not itself, is not puffed up, Doth not behave itself unseemly, seeketh not her own, is not easily provoked, thinketh no evil; Rejoiceth not in iniquity, but rejoiceth in the truth; Beareth all things, believeth all things, hopeth all things, endureth all things." This is the love that the Savior calls us to show within our families. It is a love that is willing to endure through the hard times, a love that forgives, a love that seeks the good of others above our own. The Savior gives us the ability to love in this way, and as we allow His love to flow through us, our families are strengthened and unified.

The Savior's reach into families is also a call to break the generational patterns of sin and dysfunction that often cause division. Many families struggle with patterns of behavior that have been passed down from one generation to the next—patterns of anger, addiction, unforgiveness, or control.

But the Savior has the power to break these cycles and to bring freedom and healing to families. In 2 Corinthians 5:17, we are reminded, "Therefore if any man be in Christ, he is a new creature: old things are passed away; behold, all things are become new." When the Savior reaches into a family, He brings newness—new ways of relating to one another, new patterns of love and respect, and new opportunities to live in unity. He breaks the chains of the past and sets families on a new path, one that is built on His grace and truth.

The Savior's love is the glue that holds families together. His presence brings peace to homes that are filled with tension and conflict. In Colossians 3:14-15, we are told, "And above all these things put on charity, which is the bond of perfectness. And let the peace of God rule in your hearts, to the which also ye are called in one body; and be ye thankful." The Savior's love binds families together in perfect unity, and His peace rules in the hearts of those who follow Him. When the Savior is at the center of a family, His peace fills the home, bringing an end to strife and conflict. His love creates an atmosphere where forgiveness flows freely, where grace is extended, and where each member of the family feels valued and loved. The Savior's peace is not just the absence of conflict—it is the presence of His grace, guiding every interaction and conversation, and creating a space where unity and love can flourish.

The Savior's reach into families also extends to the roles and responsibilities that each family member holds. He calls husbands and wives to love and honor one another, parents to raise their children in the knowledge and fear of the Lord, and children to honor and obey their parents. In Ephesians 5:25, husbands are called to love their wives "even as Christ also loved the church, and gave himself for it," and in Ephesians 6:1-4, children are instructed to "obey your parents in the Lord: for this is right" and fathers are told to "bring them up in the nurture and admonition of the Lord." The Savior's grace empowers each member of the family to fulfill their God-given role in a way that reflects His love and brings unity. He teaches husbands and wives how to love each other selflessly, how to communicate with respect and understanding, and how to work together as partners in raising their children. His grace also equips parents to lead their children in the ways of the Lord, providing them with the wisdom, patience, and love needed to guide their children through life's challenges. For children, the Savior's grace helps them to honor and respect their parents, recognizing the love and sacrifice that their parents have shown them. In this way, the Savior's grace brings unity to families by helping each member to fulfill their role with love and humility.

For families who have experienced deep wounds—whether through divorce, estrangement, or the loss of a loved one—the Savior's grace offers healing and hope for restoration. Even when relationships seem beyond repair, the Savior's love can rebuild what has been broken. In Psalm 147:3, we are reminded, "He healeth the broken in heart, and bindeth up their wounds." The Savior is the great healer, and He is able to mend the hearts that have been shattered by the pain of broken relationships. He brings comfort to those who are grieving, peace to those who are hurting, and hope to those who feel that reconciliation is impossible. His love has the power to restore even the most fractured families, and His grace gives us the strength to forgive, to let go of past hurts, and to rebuild relationships on the foundation of His love.

The Savior's reach into families is also a reminder that no family is perfect, but His grace is sufficient to cover every weakness, every mistake, and every failure. In 2 Corinthians 12:9, God tells us, "My grace is sufficient for thee: for my strength is made perfect in weakness." Families are made up of imperfect people, and there will always be times when we fall short, when we hurt one another, or when we fail to live up to the standards of love that the Savior has called us to. But His grace is greater than our weaknesses. His love covers our mistakes, and His strength enables us to grow, to learn, and to become the families that He has called us to be. The Savior's grace gives us the freedom to acknowledge our imperfections, to seek forgiveness, and to rely on Him for the strength to love one another as He has loved us.

In conclusion, the Savior reaches into families to restore unity and love, and His grace is the foundation upon which strong, healthy, and loving families are built. Whether a family is experiencing conflict, division, or brokenness, the Savior's love has the power to bring healing, reconciliation, and peace. He calls us to forgive one another, to love one another selflessly, and to reflect His grace in our relationships. His reach is not limited by the depth of the wounds or the length of time that a family has been divided—His love is greater than any obstacle. The Savior's grace flows into every family member, helping them to fulfill their God-given roles with love and humility, and creating an atmosphere where unity and love can flourish. No family is beyond the reach of the Savior's love, and His grace is sufficient to restore even the most broken relationships. As we invite the Savior into our families, we can trust that He will bring healing, peace, and the fullness of His love, making our families a reflection of His grace and a testimony to the power of His love.

Chapter 12 - The Savior reaches into moments of fear to provide courage and strength.

The Savior reaches into moments of fear to provide courage and strength, and there is no fear too great for His calming presence to overcome. Fear is something we all experience at different times in life—it can grip our hearts, paralyze our minds, and make us feel as though we are powerless. But in these moments, the Savior steps in with His love, which drives out fear, and with His strength, which upholds us when we feel weak. His Word reassures us that we do not have to face fear alone because He is with us every step of the way. Isaiah 41:10 offers this comforting promise: "Fear thou not; for I am with thee: be not dismayed; for I am thy God: I will strengthen thee; yea, I will help thee; yea, I will uphold thee with the right hand of my righteousness." This verse reminds us that the Savior is not distant when we are afraid; He is close, offering His strength and courage. He doesn't simply tell us not to fear; He tells us why we don't have to fear—because He is with us, and His presence is more powerful than anything we may face.

Fear can come from many sources—uncertainty about the future, the weight of responsibility, or the trials of life that seem too heavy to bear. But the Savior reaches into each of these moments, offering the courage we need to face whatever lies ahead. He understands our fears because He, too, experienced moments of fear and anguish during His time on earth. In the Garden of Gethsemane, as Jesus faced the prospect of His crucifixion, He prayed with deep sorrow and fear, saying, "O my Father, if it be possible, let this cup pass from me: nevertheless not as I will, but as thou wilt" (Matthew 26:39). Even in His darkest hour, Jesus showed us the way to face fear—with prayer, surrender, and trust in God's plan. The Savior does not minimize our fears, but He offers us the strength to endure them, just as He did. In moments when we feel overwhelmed by fear, we can follow His example by bringing our fears to God, knowing that He hears us, He cares for us, and He will provide the strength we need to keep moving forward.

When fear threatens to control our lives, the Savior's love comes to set us free. In 1 John 4:18, the Bible tells us, "There is no fear in love; but perfect love casteth out fear: because fear hath torment." The Savior's love is perfect, and it has the power to drive out the fear that torments us. Fear often stems from the unknown—what will happen next, will we have enough, will we be okay? But the Savior's love reminds us that we are secure in Him, no matter what the future holds. His love is a shield that protects our hearts from the lies that fear tells us. Fear tells us we are alone, but the Savior's love tells us we are never abandoned. Fear tells us that we are not strong enough, but the Savior's love tells us that His strength is made perfect in our weakness (2 Corinthians 12:9). Fear tells us that the future is uncertain, but the Savior's love tells us that He holds our future in His hands. His perfect love drives out fear, giving us the courage to trust Him with every aspect of our lives.

The Savior reaches into moments of fear with His peace, which is unlike anything the world can offer. In John 14:27, Jesus says, "Peace I leave with you, my peace I give unto you: not as the world giveth, give I unto you. Let not your heart be troubled, neither let it be afraid." The peace that the Savior gives is not dependent on our circumstances. It is not a fleeting feeling that comes and goes with the ups and downs of life. It is a deep, abiding peace that remains with us even in the midst of chaos, uncertainty, and fear. The world may offer temporary distractions or comforts to ease our fears, but the Savior's peace goes beyond that—it settles deep in our hearts, calming our anxious thoughts and giving us the strength to face whatever lies ahead. When we are afraid, we can turn to the Savior and ask for His peace, trusting that He will quiet our hearts and fill us with the courage we need.

In moments of fear, we often feel weak, but the Savior reaches out to strengthen us. Philippians 4:13 reminds us, "I can do all things through Christ which strengtheneth me." The strength that the Savior gives is not just physical strength; it is the inner strength to persevere, to endure, and to rise above the fear that tries to hold us back. His strength is made perfect in our weakness, and when we feel like we cannot take another step, the Savior is there to carry us. His strength sustains us in our darkest moments, giving us the courage to press on even when we are afraid. We are never meant to face fear on our own—the

Savior walks with us, and His strength becomes our strength. He does not leave us to struggle alone but empowers us to overcome fear and live in the freedom of His love and grace.

One of the most powerful examples of the Savior reaching into moments of fear to provide courage is found in the story of Peter walking on the water. In Matthew 14, the disciples were in a boat on the sea when a storm arose, and they were filled with fear. But when they saw Jesus walking toward them on the water, Peter called out, "Lord, if it be thou, bid me come unto thee on the water" (Matthew 14:28). Jesus told Peter to come, and Peter stepped out of the boat in faith. For a moment, Peter walked on the water toward Jesus, but when he saw the wind and the waves, fear gripped his heart, and he began to sink. In that moment of fear, Peter cried out, "Lord, save me," and immediately Jesus reached out His hand and caught him (Matthew 14:30-31). This story reminds us that even in moments of fear, when we feel like we are sinking, the Savior is there to reach out and lift us up. He doesn't let us drown in our fear; He reaches out with His strength and pulls us back to safety. Just as He did for Peter, the Savior offers us courage to face the storms of life, and even when we falter, He is there to catch us.

The Savior's reach into our fear is also a reminder that we are not alone. Fear often makes us feel isolated, as though we are facing our struggles on our own. But the Savior promises that He will never leave us or forsake us. In Deuteronomy 31:6, we are told, "Be strong and of a good courage, fear not, nor be afraid of them: for the Lord thy God, he it is that doth go with thee; he will not fail thee, nor forsake thee." This is the assurance we have in the Savior—He is always with us, even in our most fearful moments. We may not always feel His presence, but we can trust His promise that He is right there with us, walking beside us, carrying us when we need it, and giving us the courage to keep going. We are never alone in our fear, for the Savior is our constant companion, our refuge, and our strength.

The Savior's courage is not just about overcoming fear—it is about living boldly for Him, even in the face of challenges. In Joshua 1:9, God commands, "Have not I commanded thee? Be strong and of a good courage; be not afraid, neither be thou dismayed: for the Lord thy God is with thee whithersoever thou goest." The Savior gives us the courage to step out in faith, to pursue the calling He has placed on our lives, and to live for Him without fear of what the future may hold. When we know that the Savior is with us, we can face anything with confidence, knowing that He is in control. His courage empowers us to face our fears head-on, not because we are strong in ourselves, but because He is strong in us. The Savior's courage is a gift that enables us to live fully, to step out of the boat like Peter, and to trust that He will catch us if we begin to sink.

In moments of fear, the Savior also reaches out to remind us of His faithfulness. He has been faithful in the past, and He will be faithful in the future. In 2 Timothy 1:7, we are reminded, "For God hath not given us the spirit of fear; but of power, and of love, and of a sound mind." Fear does not come from God—it comes from the enemy, who wants to keep us paralyzed and ineffective. But the Savior has given us a spirit of power, of love, and of a sound mind. His power gives us the strength to overcome fear, His love reminds us that we are never alone, and His sound mind helps us to think clearly and make wise decisions even in the midst of fear. The Savior's faithfulness is our anchor, keeping us steady when fear tries to shake us. We can look back on His faithfulness in our lives and trust that He will continue to be faithful in every situation we face.

Ultimately, the Savior's reach into moments of fear is about transforming our hearts and minds so that we no longer live in fear, but in faith. In Romans 8:15, we are told, "For ye have not received the spirit of bondage again to fear; but ye have received the Spirit of adoption, whereby we cry, Abba, Father." The Savior has freed us from the bondage of fear, and He has adopted us as His children. As His children, we can approach Him with confidence, knowing that He is our loving Father who will protect, guide, and strengthen us. Fear no longer has a hold on us because we belong to the Savior, and His perfect love casts out all fear. When we turn to Him in our moments of fear, He reminds us of who we are in Him—His beloved children, held securely in His hands.

In conclusion, the Savior reaches into moments of fear to provide courage and strength, and His reach is greater than any fear we may face. Whether we are afraid of the future, overwhelmed by life's challenges, or struggling with uncertainty, the Savior is there to calm our hearts, strengthen our spirits, and give us the courage to keep moving forward. His love casts out fear, His peace fills our hearts, and His strength becomes our own. The Savior does not leave us to face our fears alone—He walks with us, holding us up when we feel weak and giving us the courage to trust Him in every situation. His faithfulness is our anchor, and His presence is our refuge. When we are afraid, we can turn to Him, knowing that He will always be there to provide the courage and strength we need. The Savior's reach is infinite, and His love is more powerful than any fear we may encounter. With Him by our side, we can face the future with confidence, knowing that His courage and strength will carry us through.

Chapter 13 - The Savior reaches beyond societal barriers to embrace the marginalized.

The Savior reaches beyond societal barriers to embrace the marginalized, offering His love, grace, and acceptance to those who have been overlooked, rejected, and cast aside by the world. Throughout His ministry, Jesus consistently demonstrated that His love knows no boundaries, and He defies the limitations that society places on people. He embraces the outcast, the poor, the sick, the sinner, and the foreigner, showing that every soul is precious in His sight. In a world where people are often divided by class, race, nationality, gender, and social status, the Savior steps in and breaks down those walls. He reaches across every barrier that the world creates to show that His grace is for everyone, not just for the privileged or the righteous, but for the marginalized, the broken, and the lost. Galatians 3:28 reminds us of this truth: "There is neither Jew nor Greek, there is neither bond nor free, there is neither male nor female: for ye are all one in Christ Jesus." The Savior sees beyond the external differences that often divide us, and He reaches out to embrace every person with the same love and compassion, regardless of their background or circumstances.

Jesus' earthly ministry is filled with examples of Him reaching out to the marginalized, crossing societal boundaries that others would not dare to cross. One of the most powerful examples is His encounter with the Samaritan woman at the well in John 4. Samaritans were despised by the Jews, and it was highly unusual for a Jewish man to speak to a Samaritan woman. Yet, Jesus not only spoke to her, but He treated her with dignity and respect, offering her the living water of eternal life. He looked beyond her status as an outcast and saw her heart. He didn't reject her because of her ethnicity, her gender, or her past sins. Instead, He offered her grace, forgiveness, and a new beginning. Through this simple act of kindness, Jesus showed that no one is beyond the reach of

His love. He broke through the barriers of prejudice and hatred, reaching out to someone who had been marginalized by society, and offered her the greatest gift of all—salvation.

The Savior's heart is always for the marginalized, for those who have been pushed to the edges of society, whether because of their poverty, their sins, their illness, or their social status. In Matthew 9:12-13, Jesus said, "They that be whole need not a physician, but they that are sick. But go ye and learn what that meaneth, I will have mercy, and not sacrifice: for I am not come to call the righteous, but sinners to repentance." Jesus makes it clear that His mission is to reach those who are in the greatest need, those who are broken, wounded, and weighed down by the burdens of life. He doesn't seek out the self-righteous or those who think they have it all together; He seeks out the marginalized, those who have been rejected by others, and He offers them mercy and grace. His love is for the lost, the lonely, and the forgotten, and He reaches out to them with open arms, offering healing, forgiveness, and hope.

Throughout the Gospels, we see Jesus consistently challenging the social norms of His time by embracing those whom society had cast aside. He reached out to lepers, who were considered untouchable and were forced to live in isolation. In Matthew 8:2-3, a leper came to Jesus and said, "Lord, if thou wilt, thou canst make me clean." Jesus, moved with compassion, did something unthinkable in that culture—He reached out and touched the man, saying, "I will; be thou clean." In that moment, Jesus broke the barrier of fear and prejudice, showing that His love and healing power are not limited by societal rules. He didn't see the leper as someone to be avoided or feared; He saw him as a person in need of compassion and healing. This act of love demonstrated that no one is too unclean, too sinful, or too far gone for the Savior to reach. He reaches into the lives of the marginalized, those whom others avoid or reject, and He restores their dignity, their health, and their hope.

The Savior's reach is not just for those who are physically marginalized, but also for those who are spiritually marginalized—those who feel far from God because of their sins or their failures. In Luke 19, we read the story of Zacchaeus, a tax collector who was despised by his community because of his dishonest profession. Zacchaeus was considered a traitor and a sinner, yet when Jesus passed through his town, He didn't ignore him or judge him. Instead, He called Zacchaeus by name and invited Himself to his house. In Luke 19:5, Jesus said, "Zacchaeus, make haste, and come down; for to day I must abide at thy house." This simple act of reaching out to Zacchaeus, a man who was rejected by his own people, changed his life forever. Jesus' willingness to associate with someone who was considered a sinner showed that His love and forgiveness are available to everyone, regardless of their past. Zacchaeus responded to Jesus' grace by repenting and turning his life around, and Jesus declared in Luke 19:9, "This day is salvation come to this house." The Savior reaches beyond the barriers of sin and shame, offering forgiveness and new life to those who feel unworthy of His love.

The Savior's reach is also seen in His compassion for the poor and the oppressed. In Luke 4:18, Jesus declared the purpose of His ministry: "The Spirit of the Lord is upon me, because he hath anointed me to preach the gospel to the poor; he hath sent me to heal the brokenhearted, to preach deliverance to the captives, and recovering of sight to the blind, to set at liberty them that are bruised." Jesus came to bring good news to the poor, to heal those who are hurting, and to set free those who are trapped in oppression. He didn't come for the wealthy or the powerful, but for those who had been marginalized by society—the poor, the broken, and the oppressed. He reached out to those who had nothing to offer Him in return, showing that His love is not based on what we can give Him, but on His boundless grace. He came to bring freedom and healing to those who had been overlooked, reminding them that they are deeply loved and valued by God.

One of the most profound ways the Savior reaches beyond societal barriers is through His death on the cross. In His sacrifice, He tore down the ultimate barrier—the barrier between God and humanity. Ephesians 2:13-14 says, "But now in Christ Jesus ye who sometimes were far off are made nigh by the blood of Christ. For he is our peace, who hath made both one, and hath broken down the middle wall of partition between us." Through His death, Jesus reconciled us to God and to one another, breaking down the walls of division that separate us. No longer are we defined by our social status, our race, or our sins. In Christ, we are made one, and His love embraces every person, regardless of who they are or where they come from. The cross is the ultimate demonstration of the Savior's reach beyond societal barriers, for it shows that His love is for all people, and that through Him, we are all equal and loved in the eyes of God.

The Savior's reach also extends to the foreigner and the stranger, those who are often marginalized because they are seen as different or out of place. In the parable of the Good Samaritan (Luke 10:30-37), Jesus tells the story of a man who was beaten and left for dead on the side of the road. While a priest and a Levite passed by without helping, it was a Samaritan—someone from a despised group—who stopped to care for the man. Jesus used this parable to teach that love and compassion should not be limited by societal or ethnic boundaries. The Samaritan reached out to help someone who was in need, regardless of the divisions that society had placed between them. Jesus' message is clear: We are called to love and care for everyone, especially those who are marginalized or viewed as outsiders. The Savior Himself sets the example, reaching out to embrace those who are different, those who are foreign, and those who are rejected, showing that His love knows no borders.

In Matthew 25:40, Jesus says, "Verily I say unto you, Inasmuch as ye have done it unto one of the least of these my brethren, ye have done it unto me." The Savior identifies with the marginalized, the "least of these," and He calls us to do the same. When we reach out to help the poor, the hungry, the stranger, or the prisoner, we are reaching out to Jesus Himself. The Savior's love for the marginalized is so great that He considers every act of kindness done to them as an act of love toward Him. He values the marginalized, not because of their status, but because they are made in the image of God and are deeply loved by Him.

In conclusion, the Savior reaches beyond societal barriers to embrace the marginalized, offering His love, grace, and acceptance to all. His ministry was marked by His willingness to cross every boundary, to reach out to those who had been rejected, and to bring hope and healing to those who had been cast aside. The Savior's love is for everyone, regardless of their status, race, or past, and He calls us to follow His example by loving and embracing the marginalized in our own lives. His reach is infinite, His love is boundless, and His grace is available to all who come to Him. The Savior's heart is for the outcast, the sinner, the poor, and the oppressed, and He offers them the same love, forgiveness, and salvation that He offers to everyone. Through His life, death, and resurrection, the Savior has broken down every barrier, and in Him, we are all one, united in His love and grace.

Chapter 14 - The Savior reaches into moments of failure to offer new beginnings.

The Savior reaches into moments of failure to offer new beginnings, and His grace is immeasurable in those moments when we feel like we've fallen too far. Failure has a way of crushing our spirits, filling us with guilt, shame, and a sense of hopelessness, as if the mistakes we've made define who we are and trap us in a place where we can't see a way forward. But when the weight of failure feels like too much to bear, it is the Savior who steps into the mess, into the brokenness, and lifts us out of the pit we've found ourselves in. He doesn't wait for us to fix ourselves; He comes to us right in the middle of our worst moments, reaching out with mercy and offering us something we could never earn—His forgiveness and the chance to start over. As 2 Corinthians 5:17 declares, "Therefore if any man be in Christ, he is a new creature: old things are passed away; behold, all things are become new." The old things—our failures, our regrets, our mistakes—are not the end of the story. Through Christ, they are wiped clean, and we are given a new beginning, a fresh start, a chance to walk in the fullness of His grace and forgiveness. The Savior's love reaches into the deepest places of our brokenness, and where we see only failure, He sees the potential for restoration and renewal.

We often believe that our failures define us, that they are the final word in our lives, but the Savior's reach proves otherwise. He is the God of second chances, and no matter how far we've fallen, no matter how many times we've messed up, His grace is always sufficient. Lamentations 3:22-23 gives us a beautiful reminder: "It is of the LORD's mercies that we are not consumed, because his compassions fail not. They are new every morning: great is thy faithfulness." Each morning, the Savior offers us new mercies. His faithfulness to us doesn't waver, even when we've failed. Every day is a new opportunity to receive His grace, to experience His love, and to walk in the newness of life that

He gives. The Savior doesn't hold our past mistakes against us; He invites us to leave them behind and to step into the new beginning He offers with each new day. His compassion is endless, and He never tires of giving us another chance. This is the heart of the Savior—His love is greater than our failures, and He delights in showing us mercy.

Throughout the Bible, we see time and time again how the Savior reaches into moments of failure to offer new beginnings. One of the most powerful examples is the story of Peter, the disciple who denied Jesus three times on the night of His arrest. Peter, who had been so confident in his devotion to Jesus, found himself failing in the most critical moment, denying the One he loved out of fear and self-preservation. The weight of that failure must have been overwhelming, filling him with guilt and regret. But after Jesus' resurrection, He didn't leave Peter in that place of shame. Instead, He sought Peter out, not to condemn him, but to restore him. In John 21, we see Jesus gently asking Peter three times, "Lovest thou me?" and with each response, Jesus reinstates Peter, saying, "Feed my sheep." Jesus gave Peter a new beginning, restoring him to his place as a leader among the disciples and reaffirming His love for him. This is what the Savior does for us—He reaches into the moments of our greatest failure and offers us a second chance. He doesn't focus on the failure itself; He focuses on the future He has for us, filled with His grace and purpose.

The Savior's ability to offer new beginnings is rooted in His understanding of our weaknesses. He knows that we are not perfect, that we will stumble and fall, and yet He loves us still. Hebrews 4:15 reminds us, "For we have not an high priest which cannot be touched with the feeling of our infirmities; but was in all points tempted like as we are, yet without sin." Jesus knows what it is like to face temptation, to struggle with human frailty. Though He never sinned, He understands the pressures we face, and because of that, He is full of compassion when we fail. He doesn't meet our failures with judgment or harshness; instead, He meets them with grace. He understands our humanity, and He reaches out to us with a heart full of love, ready to help us rise from the ashes of our mistakes and start anew. His grace covers our failures, and His strength is made perfect in our weakness (2 Corinthians 12:9).

The Savior's offer of new beginnings is not just about erasing the past; it's about transforming us from the inside out. When we bring our failures to Him, He doesn't just patch us up and send us on our way. He makes us new. Ezekiel

36:26 beautifully expresses this transformation: "A new heart also will I give you, and a new spirit will I put within you: and I will take away the stony heart out of your flesh, and I will give you an heart of flesh." The Savior doesn't just forgive our failures; He changes us. He takes our hardened hearts, hearts that have been shaped by sin, regret, and disappointment, and He replaces them with hearts that are soft, responsive, and open to His love. He gives us a new spirit, one that is in tune with His will and His purposes for our lives. Our failures no longer define us because the Savior has given us a new identity, one that is rooted in His grace and love.

Sometimes, after we've failed, it can be hard to believe that we deserve a new beginning. We may feel unworthy, convinced that we've messed up too many times or that our mistakes are too big for God to forgive. But the Savior's love is not based on what we deserve—it's based on His grace. Ephesians 2:8-9 reminds us, "For by grace are ye saved through faith; and that not of yourselves: it is the gift of God: not of works, lest any man should boast." The new beginnings the Savior offers are not something we can earn; they are a gift, freely given because of His great love for us. No matter how many times we've failed, the Savior's grace is always greater. He offers us forgiveness and the chance to start over, not because we've done anything to deserve it, but because He loves us unconditionally. His grace covers every failure, every sin, and every regret, giving us the freedom to move forward without being weighed down by the past.

The Savior's reach into moments of failure is a reminder that failure is not the end of our story. In fact, He often uses our failures as the starting point for something new and beautiful. Romans 8:28 assures us, "And we know that all things work together for good to them that love God, to them who are the called according to his purpose." The Savior can take even our worst mistakes and turn them into something good. He redeems our failures, using them to teach us, to strengthen us, and to draw us closer to Him. When we place our failures in His hands, He can turn them into stepping stones that lead us to a deeper relationship with Him and to the new beginnings He has in store for us. What we see as the end, He sees as the beginning of something greater.

In the Savior's hands, failure becomes an opportunity for growth and transformation. He doesn't expect us to be perfect; He knows we will stumble and fall. But instead of leaving us in our failure, He invites us to bring it to Him, to trust Him with our brokenness, and to allow Him to work in and through it. His grace is sufficient for us, and His strength is made perfect in our weakness (2 Corinthians 12:9). The Savior is not discouraged by our failures; instead, He sees them as opportunities to demonstrate His grace and power in our lives. When we are weak, He is strong. When we fall, His grace lifts us up and gives us the strength to keep going.

The Savior's offer of new beginnings is also a reflection of His unconditional love. Romans 8:38-39 declares, "For I am persuaded, that neither death, nor life, nor angels, nor principalities, nor powers, nor things present, nor things to come, nor height, nor depth, nor any other creature, shall be able to separate us from the love of God, which is in Christ Jesus our Lord." Our failures cannot separate us from the love of the Savior. His love for us is constant, unshakable, and unconditional. Even when we feel unworthy, even when we feel like we've messed up beyond repair, His love remains the same. His love is what gives us the courage to face our failures and to move forward into the new beginnings He offers. In His love, we find the freedom to leave the past behind and to embrace the future with hope.

The Savior's reach into our moments of failure is a reminder of His redemptive power. He doesn't just erase our mistakes; He redeems them. Joel 2:25 gives us a powerful promise: "And I will restore to you the years that the locust hath eaten." The Savior can restore what has been lost through our failures. He can redeem the time we feel we've wasted, the opportunities we've missed, and the relationships we've broken. He is a God of restoration, and no failure is too great for Him to redeem. In His hands, our failures become testimonies of His grace, His mercy, and His faithfulness. He takes what is broken and makes it whole again, offering us new beginnings that are even more beautiful than what we had before.

In conclusion, the Savior reaches into moments of failure to offer new beginnings, and His grace is always sufficient. No matter how many times we've failed, no matter how far we've fallen, the Savior's love and forgiveness are always available to us. He doesn't define us by our failures; He defines us by His love and the new life He offers in Him. Through His grace, He gives us the chance to begin again, to leave behind our mistakes, and to walk in the freedom of His forgiveness. The Savior's reach is infinite, and His offer of new beginnings is a constant invitation to trust Him with our failures, knowing that

He can turn them into something beautiful. In His hands, our failures become opportunities for growth, transformation, and deeper intimacy with Him. He is the God of second chances, and His love never fails.

Chapter 15 - The Savior reaches into every generation to call His people to Himself.

The Savior reaches into every generation to call His people to Himself, and His voice echoes through the ages, speaking with the same love and authority to each heart, no matter the time, place, or circumstances. From the beginning of creation to the end of time, the Savior has been drawing people to Himself, extending His hand of grace and mercy to every man, woman, and child across the centuries. His reach is not limited by time, culture, or history, but it transcends all barriers, calling out to every generation with the same invitation: to come and know Him, to find life in Him, and to walk in the purpose He has for each of us. His call is timeless, stretching from the moment He formed Adam and Eve in the garden, to the birth of the church in the book of Acts, to the hearts of every generation that has ever lived. Hebrews 13:8 declares, "Jesus Christ the same yesterday, and to day, and for ever." This truth reassures us that the same Savior who called the disciples two thousand years ago, who transformed lives in the pages of Scripture, is the same Savior who reaches out to us today, calling us to follow Him, to find rest for our souls, and to live in the freedom of His love.

In each generation, the Savior calls people out of darkness and into His marvelous light, offering the gift of salvation to all who will receive it. His love is not reserved for one specific group of people or one time in history, but for all people across all time. John 12:32 tells us, "And I, if I be lifted up from the earth, will draw all men unto me." When Jesus was lifted up on the cross, His sacrifice became the universal call for all generations to come to Him. He draws all men to Himself—young and old, rich and poor, from every nation and every era. No generation is excluded from His invitation, and no one is beyond His reach. From the days of the Old Testament prophets to the present, the Savior has been calling people to turn from sin and to receive His grace, and that call continues to this very moment, touching the hearts of people in every corner of the world.

Throughout history, we see how the Savior has faithfully reached into each generation, speaking to people in ways that they could understand, meeting them where they were, and leading them to Himself. In the days of Moses, He called the children of Israel out of slavery in Egypt, leading them through the wilderness and into the Promised Land. In Exodus 3:10, God said to Moses, "Come now therefore, and I will send thee unto Pharaoh, that thou mayest bring forth my people the children of Israel out of Egypt." The Savior's call to deliverance was not just for Moses' generation, but for all who would trust in Him. He led them with a pillar of cloud by day and a pillar of fire by night, guiding them to freedom, just as He leads us today through His Spirit, calling us out of the bondage of sin and into the freedom of His love.

In the days of the prophets, the Savior continued to call His people back to Him, even when they had wandered far from His ways. Through the voices of men like Isaiah, Jeremiah, and Ezekiel, He called out to a rebellious and broken people, offering them the hope of redemption and restoration. In Isaiah 55:6-7, the Lord pleads with His people, "Seek ye the LORD while he may be found, call ye upon him while he is near: Let the wicked forsake his way, and the unrighteous man his thoughts: and let him return unto the LORD, and he will have mercy upon him; and to our God, for he will abundantly pardon." This message of repentance and mercy was not just for Isaiah's time—it echoes down through the generations, calling us even today to turn to the Savior, to seek Him while He may be found, and to receive His abundant pardon. His reach is as close to us now as it was to the people of Israel, and His desire for us to return to Him has never changed.

When Jesus walked the earth, He continued this timeless call, reaching into the hearts of the people of His generation and inviting them to follow Him. Whether it was the fishermen on the shores of Galilee, the tax collectors sitting at their booths, or the broken and weary souls who came to Him for healing, the Savior's call was the same: "Come unto me, all ye that labour and are heavy laden, and I will give you rest" (Matthew 11:28). This invitation was not limited to those who saw Him in person; it extends to every generation that has followed, including ours. The Savior's call is personal, individual, and direct. He calls each of us by name, just as He called His disciples, and His voice still rings with the same love and authority, urging us to come to Him, to lay down our burdens, and to find rest for our souls in His presence.

The Savior's reach into every generation is also seen in the Great Commission, where He commands His followers to go into all the world and make disciples of every nation. In Matthew 28:19-20, Jesus says, "Go ye therefore, and teach all nations, baptizing them in the name of the Father, and of the Son, and of the Holy Ghost: Teaching them to observe all things whatsoever I have commanded you: and, lo, I am with you alway, even unto the end of the world." The Savior's command to spread the Gospel ensures that His call will continue to reach every generation until the end of time. Through the faithful witness of His followers, the Savior's message of love, grace, and redemption has been passed down from generation to generation, touching the lives of people in every corner of the globe. His call is not just for the past; it is for the present and the future, and it will continue until His return.

Even today, the Savior is calling out to this generation, just as He has called to every generation before us. He sees the brokenness, the confusion, and the struggles of our time, and His heart is still filled with compassion for His people. Just as He wept over Jerusalem, longing for them to turn to Him, He weeps for those in our generation who have yet to answer His call. In Matthew 23:37, Jesus said, "O Jerusalem, Jerusalem, thou that killest the prophets, and stonest them which are sent unto thee, how often would I have gathered thy children together, even as a hen gathereth her chickens under her wings, and ye would not!" The Savior's longing for His people to come to Him has not changed. He still desires to gather us under His wings, to protect us, to heal us, and to give us the life that only He can offer. His call to this generation is just as urgent as it was in the days of old, and He continues to reach out, offering His love and salvation to all who will receive it.

The Savior's call is not just for individuals—it is for families, communities, and entire nations. He desires that entire generations would come to know Him and walk in His ways. In Psalm 100:5, we are reminded of the generational nature of His love: "For the LORD is good; his mercy is everlasting; and his truth endureth to all generations." The Savior's truth is not confined to one era or one culture; it endures through all generations. His mercy is everlasting, and His faithfulness reaches from generation to generation, ensuring that His people will always have the opportunity to know Him, to experience His love, and to live in the fullness of His grace. The Savior's reach extends to our children, to their children, and to every future generation, calling them to Himself with the same love and compassion that has marked His relationship with humanity from the very beginning.

In every generation, there are those who answer the Savior's call and those who turn away. But the Savior never stops reaching out, never stops calling, and never gives up on His people. His heart is for every person in every generation to know Him and to be saved. 1 Timothy 2:4 tells us that God "will have all men to be saved, and to come unto the knowledge of the truth." The Savior's desire is that no one would be lost, that no generation would be left behind. He continues to call out, through His Word, through His Spirit, and through the testimony of His people, inviting every heart to respond to His love and to receive the gift of eternal life. His call is persistent, patient, and full of grace, and it will continue until the end of time.

In conclusion, the Savior reaches into every generation to call His people to Himself, and His call is as strong and clear today as it was in the days of the prophets, the apostles, and the early church. His love is unchanging, His mercy is everlasting, and His desire is that every person, in every generation, would come to know Him and find life in His name. The Savior's reach is not limited by time, culture, or geography—He calls all people, in every era, to come to Him, to receive His grace, and to walk in the new life He offers. As we listen for His voice and respond to His call, we become part of the great story of redemption that spans the generations, a story that began in the heart of God and will continue into eternity. The Savior's reach is infinite, His love is boundless, and His call is for all who will listen, in every generation, to come and find life, hope, and salvation in Him.

Chapter 16 - The Savior reaches into prisons of shame and guilt to set the captives free.

The Savior reaches into prisons of shame and guilt to set the captives free, breaking the chains that hold us in the darkness of our past mistakes, failures, and sins. His love is so powerful and His grace so overwhelming that no prison can keep Him out. Shame and guilt can feel like a suffocating weight, trapping us in a cycle of regret and hopelessness, convincing us that we are unworthy of forgiveness, unworthy of love, and unworthy of a second chance. But the Savior doesn't turn away from us in our moments of deepest despair—He moves toward us with compassion, reaching into the very depths of our brokenness to bring freedom and healing. In Isaiah 61:1, a prophecy about Jesus, we are told, "The Spirit of the Lord GOD is upon me; because the LORD hath anointed me to preach good tidings unto the meek; he hath sent me to bind up the brokenhearted, to proclaim liberty to the captives, and the opening of the prison to them that are bound." This is the mission of the Savior—to proclaim freedom to those who are trapped, to open the doors of the prison that guilt and shame have built around our hearts, and to lead us into the glorious liberty of His forgiveness and grace.

Shame is a powerful force that can keep us isolated from God and from others, whispering lies into our minds that we are too far gone, too stained by our sins to ever be redeemed. Guilt constantly reminds us of our wrongs, making us feel like prisoners to our past, unable to move forward. But the Savior's reach is not limited by the walls of guilt and shame that we have built. He comes to us with a heart full of mercy and a hand extended in grace, offering us the freedom that only He can give. Romans 8:1 reassures us of this truth: "There is therefore now no condemnation to them which are in Christ Jesus, who walk not after the flesh, but after the Spirit." In Christ, there is no condemnation. The guilt that once defined us, the shame that once imprisoned us, is erased by His blood. The Savior reaches into our hearts and reminds us that we are not condemned, that our sins have been forgiven, and that we are free to walk in the newness of life that He has given us.

The prison of shame is one that many of us know all too well. It is the place where we hide our true selves, where we feel unworthy of love, acceptance, and grace. It is a place of isolation and darkness, where we believe the lie that our sins and failures make us unlovable. But the Savior knows the truth about who we are, and He reaches into the prison of shame to speak life and truth into our hearts. In 1 John 1:9, we are given this incredible promise: "If we confess our sins, he is faithful and just to forgive us our sins, and to cleanse us from all unrighteousness." The Savior doesn't leave us in our shame. When we confess our sins to Him, He is faithful to forgive us and to cleanse us. He doesn't just forgive the surface-level sins; He cleanses us from all unrighteousness, reaching into the deepest places of our guilt and shame and washing them away completely. The prison walls crumble under the power of His forgiveness, and we are set free to live in the light of His grace.

One of the most beautiful aspects of the Savior's reach into our prisons of guilt and shame is that He doesn't just open the door and leave us to find our way out—He walks into the prison with us, takes us by the hand, and leads us out. He knows how heavy the weight of shame can be, and He knows how hard it can be to let go of the guilt that we've carried for so long. But He doesn't ask us to carry it alone. In Matthew 11:28-30, Jesus gives us this invitation: "Come unto me, all ye that labour and are heavy laden, and I will give you rest. Take my yoke upon you, and learn of me; for I am meek and lowly in heart: and ye shall find rest unto your souls. For my yoke is easy, and my burden is light." The Savior invites us to come to Him, to lay down the heavy burdens of guilt and shame that we've been carrying, and to find rest in His presence. He takes our burdens and replaces them with His peace, His joy, and His freedom. In the prison of guilt, we are weighed down by the constant reminder of our sins, but the Savior lifts that weight off our shoulders and gives us the freedom to walk in His love.

Throughout the Bible, we see countless examples of the Savior reaching into the prisons of guilt and shame to set people free. One of the most powerful stories is that of the woman caught in adultery in John 8. The religious leaders brought her to Jesus, ready to condemn her and stone her for her sin. But instead of joining in their condemnation, Jesus knelt down and wrote in the dust, and then He said to her accusers, "He that is without sin among you, let him first cast a stone at her." One by one, the accusers left, and Jesus was left alone with the woman. Instead of condemning her, He offered her forgiveness and a new beginning. He said to her, "Neither do I condemn thee: go, and sin no more" (John 8:11). In that moment, the prison of shame that had surrounded her was shattered by the Savior's words of grace. He didn't ignore her sin, but He didn't define her by it, either. He set her free from the guilt and shame that had held her captive, offering her the chance to walk in freedom and to live a new life. This is what the Savior does for each of us—He reaches into the moments when we feel most condemned, when we are weighed down by the guilt of our sins, and He speaks words of forgiveness and freedom over us.

Guilt can often make us feel like we are beyond redemption, that our sins are too great for the Savior to forgive. But the truth is that no sin is too great for the Savior's grace. In Psalm 103:12, we are given this beautiful promise: "As far as the east is from the west, so far hath he removed our transgressions from us." The Savior doesn't just forgive our sins; He removes them completely, casting them as far as the east is from the west. When we are trapped in the prison of guilt, it's easy to believe that our sins are always hanging over us, that we are defined by the worst things we've done. But the Savior reaches in and removes the record of our sins, setting us free to live in the freedom of His forgiveness. He doesn't hold our sins against us; instead, He washes them away completely, giving us a fresh start and a new identity in Him.

The Savior's reach into our prisons of shame and guilt is a demonstration of His incredible love and compassion for us. He doesn't leave us to wallow in our guilt or to be consumed by our shame—He comes to us with open arms, offering us the freedom that only He can give. In Luke 4:18, Jesus declares His mission: "The Spirit of the Lord is upon me, because he hath anointed me to preach the gospel to the poor; he hath sent me to heal the brokenhearted, to preach deliverance to the captives, and recovering of sight to the blind, to set at liberty them that are bruised." Jesus came to set the captives free, to break the chains of guilt and shame that keep us imprisoned, and to lead us into the light of His love and grace. His mission is to heal our broken hearts, to deliver us from the captivity of our past sins, and to give us the freedom to live in the fullness of His love.

The Savior's reach is not limited by the severity of our sins or the depth of our shame. His grace is greater than all our sins, and His love is strong enough to break through any prison that guilt and shame have built around us. In Romans 8:38-39, we are given this powerful assurance: "For I am persuaded, that neither death, nor life, nor angels, nor principalities, nor powers, nor things present, nor things to come, nor height, nor depth, nor any other creature, shall be able to separate us from the love of God, which is in Christ Jesus our Lord." Nothing can separate us from the love of the Savior—not our past, not our sins, not our guilt, and not our shame. His love reaches into every dark corner of our lives, into every prison we've found ourselves in, and He brings the light of His grace to set us free. We are never too far gone for His love to reach us, and we are never too broken for His grace to restore us.

In conclusion, the Savior reaches into prisons of shame and guilt to set the captives free, offering us the gift of forgiveness, healing, and new life. His love is greater than our sins, and His grace is more powerful than the guilt and shame that try to keep us imprisoned. The Savior's reach is infinite, and His desire is to see us walk in the freedom that only He can give. He opens the doors of the prison that guilt and shame have built around us, and He leads us into the light of His love, where we are no longer defined by our past but by His grace. In Him, there is no condemnation, and we are free to live in the fullness of His forgiveness and love. The Savior's mission is to set the captives free, and no matter how deep the prison of guilt and shame may feel, His reach is always enough to bring us into the glorious liberty of His grace.

Chapter 17 - The Savior reaches into the lives of the lost to offer guidance and direction.

The Savior reaches into the lives of the lost to offer guidance and direction, His love extending far beyond the darkness of confusion and wandering, to lead each one of us to the path of life, hope, and truth. Being lost can feel overwhelming, like wandering through a maze with no clear way out. Whether we are lost because of our own choices, led astray by sin, or simply confused by the complexities of life, the Savior sees us. He sees our struggles, our fears, and our uncertainties, and in His infinite compassion, He reaches down to offer His hand, ready to guide us back to Himself. In Luke 19:10, Jesus says, "For the Son of man is come to seek and to save that which was lost." This simple yet powerful truth captures the heart of the Savior's mission—He is a seeker of the lost, a Savior who goes into the dark and desolate places to find us, to rescue us, and to guide us into His light. No matter how far we've strayed, how lost we feel, or how hopeless our situation seems, the Savior never stops searching for us. His reach is long, His love is wide, and He is relentless in His pursuit of the lost.

The lost are those who have drifted from the truth, who have wandered far from God's plan, but the Savior's love is so great that He doesn't leave us in that lost state. He steps into our confusion, offering not only a way out but also a way forward. Proverbs 3:5-6 reminds us of the guidance He provides: "Trust in the LORD with all thine heart; and lean not unto thine own understanding. In all thy ways acknowledge him, and he shall direct thy paths." When we feel lost and unsure of which way to turn, the Savior invites us to trust Him completely. He calls us to stop relying on our own limited understanding, to surrender our need to control the outcome, and to place our lives fully in His hands. When we do this, He promises to direct our paths, to show us the way we should go, and to lead us toward the life He has prepared for us. The Savior's guidance is not based on human wisdom or the fleeting opinions of the world; it is grounded in His perfect knowledge, His eternal truth, and His deep love for each of us.

Being lost can look different for different people. For some, it is a spiritual lostness—a feeling of separation from God, a sense of wandering in a wilderness of doubt and sin. For others, it is the confusion that comes from life's many challenges: decisions about the future, uncertainty about relationships, or fear of failure. But no matter the reason for our lostness, the Savior's response is always the same: He reaches out to guide us. Psalm 32:8 offers us this comforting promise: "I will instruct thee and teach thee in the way which thou shalt go: I will guide thee with mine eye." The Savior doesn't just point us in the right direction from afar—He walks with us every step of the way, teaching us, instructing us, and guiding us with His loving eye. He is not a distant guide who leaves us to figure things out on our own; He is a close and caring Shepherd who leads us gently along the path, ensuring that we are never alone as we find our way.

One of the most powerful images of the Savior's guidance is found in Psalm 23, where David describes the Lord as his Shepherd. In verses 1-3, David writes, "The LORD is my shepherd; I shall not want. He maketh me to lie down in green pastures: he leadeth me beside the still waters. He restoreth my soul: he leadeth me in the paths of righteousness for his name's sake." The Savior is not just any guide; He is the Good Shepherd, who leads His sheep to places of peace, rest, and restoration. When we are lost, weary, and overwhelmed, the Savior doesn't push us forward in fear or force us down the path. Instead, He leads us with kindness and patience, guiding us to the still waters where our souls can be refreshed. He restores what has been broken, and He leads us in the right paths, not because we are deserving, but for His name's sake—because of His great love and mercy.

Jesus' parable of the lost sheep in Luke 15:4-7 paints a vivid picture of the Savior's heart for the lost. He tells of a shepherd who, despite having ninety-nine sheep safe in the fold, goes after the one sheep that is lost. The shepherd doesn't wait for the lost sheep to find its way back; instead, he goes out into the wilderness, searching until he finds it. And when he finds it, he carries it back on his shoulders, rejoicing. This is the heart of the Savior—He doesn't give up on the lost. Even when we feel far from God, even when we've wandered away, the Savior actively seeks us, pursuing us with relentless love. He finds us in our lostness, and He doesn't scold or shame us for straying. Instead, He lifts us up, carries us on His shoulders, and brings us back into the safety of His fold. His joy is complete when the lost are found, and He celebrates every soul that turns back to Him.

The Savior's guidance is not just for the big moments in life; it is for the everyday decisions and struggles we face. Psalm 119:105 reminds us, "Thy word is a lamp unto my feet, and a light unto my path." The Savior's Word is our guide in the darkness, a light that illuminates the path before us so that we can see the next step to take. When we are lost in confusion, when the way forward seems unclear, we can turn to His Word for direction. His Word is full of wisdom, truth, and promises that provide the clarity we need to navigate life's challenges. The Savior doesn't leave us to wander aimlessly in the dark—He has given us His Word as a beacon of light to guide us toward the truth, toward Him, and toward the life He has planned for us.

Sometimes, the lostness we experience is a result of our own sin and rebellion. We may have turned away from God, choosing to follow our own path instead of His. In those moments, it can feel like we've gone too far, that we've lost our way beyond recovery. But even then, the Savior reaches out to guide us back to Himself. Isaiah 30:21 offers this promise: "And thine ears shall hear a word behind thee, saying, This is the way, walk ye in it, when ye turn to the right hand, and when ye turn to the left." Even when we've strayed, the Savior speaks to us, calling us back to the right path. He doesn't abandon us to the consequences of our choices; instead, He lovingly corrects us, guiding us back to the way of righteousness. His guidance is not harsh or condemning—it is full of grace, drawing us back to the life and purpose He has for us.

The Savior's reach into the lives of the lost is not limited by our circumstances or by how far we've strayed. In fact, He specializes in finding those who are the most lost. In Luke 19, we read the story of Zacchaeus, a tax collector who was despised by his community because of his corrupt practices. Zacchaeus was lost in the sense that he had chosen a life of greed and dishonesty, far from the ways of God. But when Jesus passed through Jericho, Zacchaeus was desperate to see Him, climbing a tree just to catch a glimpse. Jesus didn't pass him by; instead, He called out to Zacchaeus and said, "Zacchaeus, make haste, and come down; for to day I must abide at thy house" (Luke 19:5). That simple invitation changed Zacchaeus's life forever. Jesus reached into the life of a man who was lost in sin and offered him not only guidance but also friendship and redemption. Zacchaeus responded by turning away from his old life and making things right with those he had wronged. This is the power of the Savior's reach—He finds us in our lostness, no matter how far we've wandered, and He offers us a new way, a new life, and a new beginning.

In John 14:6, Jesus declares, "I am the way, the truth, and the life: no man cometh unto the Father, but by me." The Savior is not just a guide; He is the way. He doesn't merely point us in the right direction—He is the path we must follow. When we are lost, the answer is not to rely on our own wisdom or to search for direction in the world's ever-changing opinions. The answer is to look to Jesus, to follow Him, and to trust that He will lead us in the right way. He is the way to the Father, the way to eternal life, and the way to true peace and joy. When we place our trust in Him, He leads us out of our lostness and into the fullness of life that only He can offer.

The Savior's reach into the lives of the lost is a reflection of His deep love for each of us. He doesn't want anyone to remain lost or separated from Him. 2 Peter 3:9 tells us, "The Lord is not slack concerning his promise, as some men count slackness; but is longsuffering to us-ward, not willing that any should perish, but that all should come to repentance." The Savior's desire is that every lost soul would find its way back to Him. He is patient with us, giving us time and space to respond to His call, and

He never stops reaching out, even when we resist. His love for the lost is boundless, and His heart is always to guide us back to Himself, to the place where we belong.

In conclusion, the Savior reaches into the lives of the lost to offer guidance and direction, and His reach is always enough to bring us back to the path of life. No matter how lost we feel, no matter how far we've strayed, the Savior's love and grace are always there, ready to lead us home. He is the Good Shepherd who seeks out the lost sheep, the loving guide who walks with us through life's challenges, and the Way, the Truth, and the Life who shows us the path to the Father. His guidance is perfect, His love is relentless, and His desire is for every lost soul to find its way back to Him. When we are lost, we need only to call out to Him, and He will faithfully lead us to the life and purpose He has prepared for us.

Chapter 18 - The Savior reaches into the cries of the oppressed to bring justice and deliverance.

The Savior reaches into the cries of the oppressed to bring justice and deliverance, and His heart is moved by the pain, suffering, and injustice that weigh so heavily on the lives of those who are crushed under the burdens of this world. When we think of oppression, we think of the countless ways people are silenced, ignored, mistreated, or held down by systems, circumstances, or even individuals that seek to strip them of their dignity and worth. Whether it's physical oppression, emotional abuse, spiritual bondage, or societal injustice, the Savior hears the cries of the oppressed and moves with compassion to bring freedom, justice, and healing. In Exodus 3:7-8, God's words to Moses resonate with His unwavering care for the oppressed: "And the LORD said, I have surely seen the affliction of my people which are in Egypt, and have heard their cry by reason of their taskmasters; for I know their sorrows; and I am come down to deliver them out of the hand of the Egyptians." These words are a powerful reminder that the Savior does not turn a blind eye to suffering. He sees, He hears, and He knows every tear, every plea, and every silent cry for help. His heart is stirred by the afflictions of His people, and He steps in with divine authority to bring justice to those who have been wronged and deliverance to those who are bound.

The oppression we experience in this world can take many forms. For some, it's the weight of poverty and hunger, for others, it's the pain of discrimination or persecution. Some are oppressed by fear and anxiety, while others are trapped in cycles of addiction, abuse, or violence. But whatever the form of oppression, the Savior's response is always the same—He comes to set the captives free and to bring justice to the downtrodden. Isaiah 61:1-2 captures the essence of the Savior's mission: "The Spirit of the Lord GOD is upon me;

because the LORD hath anointed me to preach good tidings unto the meek; he hath sent me to bind up the brokenhearted, to proclaim liberty to the captives, and the opening of the prison to them that are bound; to proclaim the acceptable year of the LORD, and the day of vengeance of our God; to comfort all that mourn." This passage is not just a prophecy about Jesus; it is a declaration of His heart for the oppressed. He was anointed to bring good news to the poor, to heal the brokenhearted, to proclaim freedom to the captives, and to release those who are imprisoned by injustice and suffering.

The Savior's reach into the lives of the oppressed is both personal and powerful. He doesn't just observe from a distance or offer hollow words of comfort. He steps into the very situation, bringing His presence, His power, and His justice to bear. When we feel like our voices are lost in the noise, when we feel unseen and unheard, the Savior reminds us that He sees us, that He hears our cries, and that He is working on our behalf. Psalm 34:17 offers this assurance: "The righteous cry, and the LORD heareth, and delivereth them out of all their troubles." The Savior is near to the brokenhearted, and He does not ignore the cries of those who are in distress. His ears are always attentive to the voices of the oppressed, and His hands are ready to move in power to bring about deliverance.

Justice is not something that the Savior simply desires—it is who He is. Psalm 89:14 declares, "Justice and judgment are the habitation of thy throne: mercy and truth shall go before thy face." The foundation of the Savior's rule is justice. He cannot stand idly by while His people suffer at the hands of injustice. Throughout Scripture, we see the Savior's deep commitment to justice, not only as a concept but as a reality He works to bring about in the lives of those who have been oppressed. He is the righteous judge who will one day set all things right, and even now, He is working to bring justice to those who have been wronged. When we feel powerless in the face of injustice, the Savior reminds us that He is the ultimate source of justice, and He will not allow evil to prevail forever.

One of the most vivid examples of the Savior bringing justice and deliverance to the oppressed is found in the story of the Israelites in Egypt. For 400 years, the Israelites were enslaved, oppressed by the harsh rule of the Egyptians, crying out for freedom and deliverance. Yet, God did not forget them. He heard their cries, and He sent Moses to lead them out of slavery, performing miracles and wonders to break the chains of their oppression. In Exodus 14:13-14, Moses spoke to the people, saying, "Fear ye not, stand still, and see the salvation of the LORD, which he will shew to you to day: for the Egyptians whom ye have seen to day, ye shall see them again no more for ever. The LORD shall fight for you, and ye shall hold your peace." This moment encapsulates the Savior's heart for justice. He fights for His people when they are powerless, and He delivers them with mighty acts of salvation. The Savior's deliverance of the Israelites from Egypt is not just a historical event; it is a powerful symbol of His ability to break every form of oppression, to deliver us from the hands of our enemies, and to lead us into the freedom He has promised.

But the Savior's justice is not just about physical deliverance—it's about spiritual deliverance as well. Many of us are oppressed not only by external forces but by the internal weight of sin, guilt, and shame. The enemy of our souls seeks to keep us bound in chains of fear and condemnation, convincing us that we are unworthy of the Savior's love and grace. But the Savior reaches into even the deepest spiritual oppression, offering us freedom through His sacrifice on the cross. Colossians 1:13-14 reminds us, "Who hath delivered us from the power of darkness, and hath translated us into the kingdom of his dear Son: in whom we have redemption through his blood, even the forgiveness of sins." Through His death and resurrection, the Savior has delivered us from the power of darkness, setting us free from the oppression of sin and bringing us into His kingdom of light. His justice is not just about righting earthly wrongs—it is about setting us free from the spiritual bondage that keeps us from living in the fullness of His love and grace.

The Savior's deliverance is often described as a mighty hand that rescues His people from their enemies, but it is also a tender hand that comforts those who are hurting. In the midst of oppression, we can feel crushed, broken, and abandoned, but the Savior's reach is always there to bring comfort and healing. Psalm 147:3 tells us, "He healeth the broken in heart, and bindeth up their wounds." The Savior doesn't just deliver us from the external forces of oppression—He heals the wounds that oppression has left behind. He binds up our broken hearts, mends the pieces of our souls that have been shattered by injustice, and restores us to wholeness. His deliverance is not just about removing the oppressor—it is about bringing complete healing and restoration to those who have been oppressed.

In the New Testament, we see the Savior reaching into the lives of the oppressed with compassion and authority. One of the most powerful stories of His deliverance is found in Luke 13, where Jesus heals a woman who had been crippled by a spirit for eighteen years. She had been bent over, unable to stand up straight, oppressed by both her physical condition and the spiritual forces that had bound her. But when Jesus saw her, He called her to Him and said, "Woman, thou art loosed from thine infirmity" (Luke 13:12). With a touch, He set her free from the oppression that had held her captive for nearly two decades. This story is a reminder that the Savior's power to deliver is not limited by time, circumstance, or the depth of our oppression. Whether we have been bound for eighteen years or for a lifetime, the Savior's reach is long enough, strong enough, and compassionate enough to deliver us and set us free.

The Savior's justice is also about lifting up the voices of the oppressed, ensuring that they are heard and that their suffering is not ignored. In Proverbs 31:8-9, we are called to follow His example: "Open thy mouth for the dumb in the cause of all such as are appointed to destruction. Open thy mouth, judge righteously, and plead the cause of the poor and needy." The Savior calls us to stand with the oppressed, to speak up for those who cannot speak for themselves, and to be agents of His justice in a world that often turns a blind eye to suffering. His heart for the oppressed compels us to act, to love mercy, and to walk humbly with our God (Micah 6:8), knowing that as we work for justice, we are partnering with the Savior in His mission to bring freedom and deliverance to those who are hurting.

Ultimately, the Savior's justice will be fully realized when He returns to establish His kingdom on earth. Revelation 21:4 gives us a glimpse of this future hope: "And God shall wipe away all tears from their eyes; and there shall be no more death, neither sorrow, nor crying, neither shall there be any more pain: for the former things are passed away." In that day, all oppression will cease, and the Savior will bring perfect justice and eternal deliverance to His people. Until then, we can trust in His promise to hear our cries, to act on our behalf, and to bring justice and deliverance in His perfect timing.

In conclusion, the Savior reaches into the cries of the oppressed to bring justice and deliverance, and His heart is always for those who are suffering.

Whether we are oppressed by external forces or internal struggles, His reach is always enough to set us free. He fights for us, He heals us, and He lifts us out of the pit of oppression, placing us on the solid ground of His love and grace. His justice is perfect, His deliverance is sure, and His compassion is unending. As we cry out to Him in our moments of deepest need, we can trust that He hears us, that He is with us, and that He will bring justice and deliverance to every situation.

Chapter 19 - The Savior reaches into spiritual blindness to open the eyes of faith.

The Savior reaches into spiritual blindness to open the eyes of faith, bringing light into the darkest places of our hearts and minds, where ignorance, doubt, and sin have clouded our vision. Spiritual blindness is one of the most devastating conditions a person can experience because it leaves us unable to see the truth of God's love, unable to understand the depth of His grace, and unable to grasp the beauty of the life He offers through faith. In our blindness, we stumble through life, trying to make sense of the world, searching for meaning, and longing for something more, yet never able to find it on our own. But the Savior, in His mercy, does not leave us in this state. He comes to us, reaches into our blindness, and opens our eyes so that we can see clearly for the first time. Jesus Himself declared this as part of His mission in Luke 4:18, quoting Isaiah: "The Spirit of the Lord is upon me, because he hath anointed me to preach the gospel to the poor; he hath sent me to heal the brokenhearted, to preach deliverance to the captives, and recovering of sight to the blind." The Savior's reach is not just for physical blindness, though He healed many in His earthly ministry; it is also for those who are spiritually blind, unable to see the light of God's truth. He comes to us in our darkness, bringing the light of faith that opens our eyes and changes everything.

Spiritual blindness is the inability to see God for who He truly is, and the inability to see ourselves in the light of His truth. We are blinded by the world, by our sins, by the lies of the enemy, and by our own pride. We walk in darkness, thinking we understand life, thinking we can make our own way, but in reality, we are lost and blind. The Bible warns us about this condition in 2 Corinthians 4:4: "In whom the god of this world hath blinded the minds of them which believe not, lest the light of the glorious gospel of Christ, who is the image of God, should shine unto them." The enemy works tirelessly to keep people in spiritual darkness, blinding their minds so that they cannot see the truth of the gospel. This blindness keeps people from seeing the beauty of Christ and the salvation He offers, trapping them in a life without hope, without purpose, and without direction. But the Savior's light is more powerful than any darkness. No matter how blind we may be, no matter how lost we feel, the Savior's reach is enough to open our eyes and let His light flood in.

One of the most vivid illustrations of spiritual blindness is found in the story of the apostle Paul, who was once known as Saul. Saul was a zealous persecutor of Christians, convinced that he was doing God's will by imprisoning and even killing those who followed Jesus. He was spiritually blind, unable to see that Jesus was the Messiah, unable to understand that he was fighting against God Himself. But in Acts 9, as Saul was on his way to Damascus to arrest more Christians, the Savior reached into his blindness in a dramatic way. A bright light from heaven suddenly shone around him, and Saul fell to the ground, blinded by the glory of the Savior. Jesus spoke to him, saying, "Saul, Saul, why persecutest thou me?" (Acts 9:4). In that moment, Saul's physical blindness mirrored his spiritual blindness. He had been blind to the truth of Jesus, but now, through this divine encounter, the Savior was opening his eyes. Three days later, Saul's sight was restored when a disciple named Ananias prayed for him, and with his physical sight restored, his spiritual eyes were also opened. Saul became Paul, one of the greatest apostles, spreading the gospel of Jesus Christ to the world. This powerful transformation shows us that no one is too blind for the Savior to reach. No one is too far gone for the Savior's light to penetrate the darkness.

The Savior's ability to open the eyes of the spiritually blind is not just for those who have never known Him—it is also for believers who may have lost their way, who have become spiritually blinded by sin, distractions, or doubt. Even those who follow Jesus can experience moments of blindness, where the things of this world cloud our vision, and we lose sight of the Savior's truth. But even then, the Savior reaches into our lives, gently removing the scales from our eyes and helping us see clearly once again. In Revelation 3:18, Jesus offers this counsel to the church at Laodicea: "I counsel thee to buy of me gold tried in the fire, that thou mayest be rich; and white raiment, that thou mayest be clothed, and that the shame of thy nakedness do not appear; and anoint thine eyes with eyesalve, that thou mayest see." The Savior knows that even believers can become spiritually blind, and He offers us the healing we need to restore our spiritual sight. He anoints our eyes with the salve of His grace, opening them once again to see the beauty of His truth, to understand His will, and to follow Him with renewed clarity and purpose.

The Savior's reach into spiritual blindness is an act of His immense love. He does not leave us wandering in the darkness, stumbling through life without direction. Instead, He comes to us with compassion, offering the light of faith that can transform our lives. In John 8:12, Jesus declared, "I am the light of the world: he that followeth me shall not walk in darkness, but shall have the light of life." When we follow the Savior, He leads us out of darkness and into His marvelous light. The light of life is not just the ability to see with our physical eyes; it is the ability to see with the eyes of faith, to understand the truth of who Jesus is and what He has done for us. This light gives us direction, purpose, and hope, guiding us through the challenges of life and showing us the way to eternal life with Him.

When the Savior opens our spiritual eyes, we begin to see everything differently. We see ourselves as we truly are—sinners in need of grace, but also beloved children of God, redeemed by the blood of Christ. We see the world through His eyes, with compassion for the lost and a desire to share His love with others. We see the path that He has set before us, a path of righteousness, peace, and joy in the Holy Spirit. The Savior's light transforms not only how we see, but also how we live. In Ephesians 1:18, the apostle Paul prays, "The eyes of your understanding being enlightened; that ye may know what is the hope of his calling, and what the riches of the glory of his inheritance in the saints." When the Savior opens the eyes of our understanding, we begin to comprehend the hope to which we have been called. We understand the riches of His grace, the depth of His love, and the glory that awaits us in His kingdom. This enlightenment empowers us to live boldly, to walk in faith, and to share the light of Christ with a world that is still blinded by darkness.

The Savior's reach into spiritual blindness is not just about giving us knowledge—it's about giving us a relationship with Him. When our spiritual eyes are opened, we don't just see facts and doctrines; we see the Savior Himself. We come to know Him personally, to experience His love and His presence in our lives. In John 14:9, Jesus said to Philip, "He that hath seen me hath seen the Father." When the Savior opens our eyes, we see God in all His glory, in all

His goodness, and in all His love. We realize that the God of the universe is not distant or indifferent, but He is near, reaching out to us, inviting us into a relationship with Him. This relationship is the foundation of our faith, and it is what sustains us through all the trials and challenges of life.

One of the most profound moments of spiritual blindness and sight in the Bible is the story of the two disciples on the road to Emmaus after Jesus' resurrection. In Luke 24, we read that these two disciples were walking along the road, talking about all that had happened, but they were unable to recognize Jesus when He appeared and walked with them. They were spiritually blind, unable to see that the very Savior they were mourning was alive and standing right beside them. But as Jesus walked with them, explaining the Scriptures and breaking bread with them, their eyes were opened, and they recognized Him. Luke 24:31 says, "And their eyes were opened, and they knew him; and he vanished out of their sight." In that moment, their spiritual blindness was lifted, and they saw Jesus for who He truly was—the risen Savior, the fulfillment of all God's promises. This story reminds us that even when we don't recognize it, the Savior is walking with us, guiding us, and waiting to open our eyes so that we can see Him clearly.

The Savior's reach into spiritual blindness is an ongoing process. Even after our eyes are opened, we continue to grow in our understanding of His truth and His will. The more we walk with Him, the more clearly we see. In 2 Peter 3:18, we are encouraged to "grow in grace, and in the knowledge of our Lord and Saviour Jesus Christ." Spiritual sight is not something we receive once and then forget about—it is something we cultivate as we deepen our relationship with the Savior. Each day, He opens our eyes a little more, helping us to see more of His love, more of His truth, and more of His plans for our lives. The journey of faith is a journey of growing in spiritual sight, as the Savior continues to lead us into greater understanding and deeper intimacy with Him.

In conclusion, the Savior reaches into spiritual blindness to open the eyes of faith, bringing light, understanding, and transformation into our lives. His love is so great that He does not leave us in the darkness, but He comes to us with the light of His truth, guiding us into a relationship with Him and giving us the eyes to see the beauty of His grace. No matter how blind we may feel, no matter how lost we may be, the Savior's reach is always enough to open our eyes and lead us into the light of faith. His light is more powerful than any darkness, and

His love is more transformative than we could ever imagine. As we allow Him to open our eyes, we begin to see the world, ourselves, and the Savior Himself in a whole new way—through the eyes of faith, illuminated by His grace.

Chapter 20 - The Savior reaches across the gap between God and humanity to bring reconciliation.

The Savior reaches across the gap between God and humanity to bring reconciliation, bridging the chasm that sin created and restoring the broken relationship between a holy God and His wayward children. This divine act of love, grace, and mercy is the heart of the gospel, the very reason Jesus came to earth, lived a sinless life, died a sacrificial death, and rose again in victory. From the beginning of time, humanity has struggled with the consequences of sin, which separates us from God and leaves us distant, lost, and unable to approach Him on our own. Isaiah 59:2 says, "But your iniquities have separated between you and your God, and your sins have hid his face from you, that he will not hear." This separation is not just physical—it's spiritual, emotional, and relational. Our sins erect a wall between us and the God who created us, and no matter how hard we try, we cannot tear that wall down on our own. But the Savior, in His great love, reaches across that gap, offering Himself as the way back to God, the only bridge that can reconnect us to the One who made us, loves us, and longs to be in relationship with us.

This reconciliation is not something we can achieve by our own efforts, our own goodness, or our own deeds. It is a gift of grace, made possible by the sacrificial love of Jesus Christ. In Romans 5:10, we are reminded of the incredible truth: "For if, when we were enemies, we were reconciled to God by the death of his Son, much more, being reconciled, we shall be saved by his life." Even when we were enemies of God, lost in our sin and rebellion, the Savior reached across the divide, offering His own life as the price for our reconciliation. He didn't wait for us to clean ourselves up, to become worthy of His love, or to make the first move. He came to us, taking the initiative, bridging the gap through His death on the cross, and making peace between

God and humanity. His love for us is so great that He willingly laid down His life to restore what sin had broken, to heal the relationship that had been shattered, and to bring us back into fellowship with our Creator.

The gap between God and humanity is a gap that no human effort could ever close. From the moment sin entered the world through Adam and Eve, humanity has been separated from the fullness of God's presence. Romans 3:23 tells us, "For all have sinned, and come short of the glory of God." No one is exempt from this condition of sin. We are all born into this broken state, unable to reach God on our own. But the beauty of the gospel is that God didn't leave us in that brokenness. He sent His Son, Jesus, to stand in the gap, to be the mediator between us and God. In 1 Timothy 2:5, we read, "For there is one God, and one mediator between God and men, the man Christ Jesus." Jesus is the only one who could bridge the gap, because He is both fully God and fully man. As God, He is perfect and holy, able to stand in the presence of the Father. As man, He took on our humanity, identifying with our struggles, our pain, and our sin, yet without sinning Himself. Through His death and resurrection, Jesus became the perfect mediator, the bridge that reconnects us to God and restores the relationship that sin had severed.

The Savior's act of reconciliation is not just a legal transaction or a distant, impersonal act—it is deeply relational and rooted in His love for us. In 2 Corinthians 5:18-19, we are given a glimpse of the depth of this love: "And all things are of God, who hath reconciled us to himself by Jesus Christ, and hath given to us the ministry of reconciliation; to wit, that God was in Christ, reconciling the world unto himself, not imputing their trespasses unto them; and hath committed unto us the word of reconciliation." Through Jesus, God was not just erasing our sins from a list of wrongs; He was reconciling the world to Himself. This reconciliation is personal. It is the Father's heart longing for His children to come back to Him, to be in relationship with Him once again. When Jesus reached across the gap, He wasn't just dealing with the abstract concept of sin—He was reaching out to each of us, calling us by name, inviting us back into the arms of the Father. His death on the cross was the ultimate act of love, a love that broke through the barrier of sin and made it possible for us to be reunited with God.

The reconciliation that the Savior offers is not just about forgiveness of sins—it's about restoring the fullness of relationship with God. In Ephesians

2:13-14, Paul writes, "But now in Christ Jesus ye who sometimes were far off are made nigh by the blood of Christ. For he is our peace, who hath made both one, and hath broken down the middle wall of partition between us." The blood of Christ has brought us near to God, tearing down the wall that separated us. This nearness is what we were created for. From the very beginning, humanity was made to walk in close fellowship with God, to know Him, to love Him, and to be loved by Him. Sin destroyed that intimacy, but through Jesus, that intimacy is restored. The Savior's reach across the gap brings us back into the closeness we were always meant to have with God. It's not just about being forgiven—it's about being brought near, being welcomed into the very presence of God, where we can experience His love, His peace, and His joy in ways that we never could while we were separated from Him.

This reconciliation is not something we have to earn—it is a free gift of grace, offered to us through faith in Jesus Christ. Ephesians 2:8-9 reminds us, "For by grace are ye saved through faith; and that not of yourselves: it is the gift of God: not of works, lest any man should boast." We don't have to work our way back to God. We don't have to strive to close the gap on our own. The Savior has already done the work. He has already reached across the divide, offering us His hand and inviting us to receive the gift of reconciliation through faith in Him. All we have to do is accept it, to trust in His finished work on the cross, and to receive the new life that He offers. This is the beauty of the gospel—it's not about what we can do to reach God; it's about what Jesus has already done to reach us.

The reconciliation that the Savior brings also has a transformative effect on our lives. Once we are reconciled to God, we are called to live in the light of that reconciliation, to be ambassadors of His love and grace to the world around us. In 2 Corinthians 5:20, Paul writes, "Now then we are ambassadors for Christ, as though God did beseech you by us: we pray you in Christ's stead, be ye reconciled to God." As those who have been reconciled to God, we are now called to share that message of reconciliation with others. The Savior's reach across the gap is not just for us—it's for the whole world. He desires that all people would come to know Him, that all would be reconciled to the Father, and that the barriers that separate us from God would be torn down in every heart. As ambassadors of Christ, we carry the message of reconciliation to a world that is still lost in darkness, still separated from God, still in need of the Savior's healing touch.

The Savior's reach across the gap between God and humanity is the ultimate expression of His love and His desire for relationship with us. It's a love that is willing to go to any length, to endure any suffering, to overcome any obstacle in order to bring us back to the Father. In John 3:16, we see the depth of this love: "For God so loved the world, that he gave his only begotten Son, that whosoever believeth in him should not perish, but have everlasting life." The Savior's reach is motivated by love—a love so deep, so sacrificial, that He was willing to give His very life to close the gap that sin had created. This love is not conditional; it is not based on our performance or our worthiness. It is freely given to all who will receive it, to all who will place their faith in Jesus and trust in His work of reconciliation.

As we reflect on the Savior's reach across the gap, we are reminded that this reconciliation is not just for the future—it's for the here and now. Through Jesus, we can experience the joy of reconciliation with God in this life, walking in fellowship with Him, experiencing His presence, and living in the freedom that comes from being forgiven and restored. Romans 5:1 tells us, "Therefore being justified by faith, we have peace with God through our Lord Jesus Christ." This peace with God is the result of the reconciliation that the Savior has made possible. It's a peace that surpasses all understanding, a peace that fills our hearts and minds as we walk in relationship with God, knowing that the gap has been closed, the wall has been torn down, and we are now His beloved children.

In conclusion, the Savior reaches across the gap between God and humanity to bring reconciliation, offering us the gift of restored relationship with the Father. Through His sacrificial death on the cross, Jesus became the bridge that reconnects us to God, healing the division that sin had caused and bringing us back into the fullness of life with Him. This reconciliation is a free gift of grace, offered to all who will place their faith in

Jesus and receive the forgiveness and new life He provides. The Savior's reach is infinite, His love is boundless, and His desire is for all people to be reconciled to God. As we accept this gift and live in the light of His love, we are called to be ambassadors of reconciliation, sharing the message of His grace with a world that is still lost and in need of the Savior's healing touch. Through

Jesus, the gap has been closed, and we can now walk in the joy, peace, and freedom of being reconciled to God, both now and for all eternity.

Chapter 21 - The Savior reaches into moments of loneliness to remind us we are never alone.

The Savior reaches into moments of loneliness to remind us we are never alone, offering us comfort, peace, and the assurance of His constant presence in our lives. Loneliness can be one of the most painful and isolating feelings we experience as humans. Whether it's the loneliness that comes from physical separation, the emotional distance we feel from others, or the deep spiritual loneliness when we feel far from God, it has a way of convincing us that we are forgotten, unseen, and unloved. But in these moments of loneliness, the Savior steps in with a gentle reminder: "You are not alone. I am with you." His presence is a constant source of hope and strength, and He never leaves us, even when we feel abandoned by the world. In Matthew 28:20, Jesus gives us this beautiful promise: "Lo, I am with you always, even unto the end of the world." This is the heart of the Savior—to be with us in every moment, especially in our loneliness, reminding us that His love never leaves us, and His presence never fades.

In those times when the weight of loneliness presses down on our hearts, the Savior reaches out to us, just as He reached out to so many in the Bible who felt abandoned or forgotten. One of the most poignant stories of loneliness is found in the life of Hagar, a servant who was cast out into the wilderness with her son, feeling utterly alone and hopeless. In Genesis 21, we find her sitting by a spring of water, weeping, overwhelmed by the loneliness of her situation. But in that moment of despair, God came to her, offering her comfort and reassurance. Genesis 21:17 tells us, "And God heard the voice of the lad; and the angel of God called to Hagar out of heaven, and said unto her, What aileth thee, Hagar? Fear not; for God hath heard the voice of the lad where he is." The Savior heard Hagar's cries, and He came to remind her that she was not alone. He provided for her needs and gave her hope for the future. This is what the

Savior does for us when we feel abandoned—He steps into our loneliness, hears our cries, and assures us that He is near.

Loneliness can make us feel like no one understands what we're going through, but the Savior knows our hearts better than anyone. In Hebrews 4:15, we are reminded that "we have not an high priest which cannot be touched with the feeling of our infirmities; but was in all points tempted like as we are, yet without sin." Jesus knows what it's like to feel alone. He experienced loneliness during His time on earth, particularly in the Garden of Gethsemane, where He prayed in anguish, feeling the weight of the world's sins upon Him. As He prayed, His disciples slept, and He was left to face His sorrow alone. In Matthew 26:38, Jesus said to them, "My soul is exceeding sorrowful, even unto death: tarry ye here, and watch with me." In that moment, Jesus felt the depth of loneliness, yet He turned to the Father for strength. Even on the cross, when He cried out, "My God, my God, why hast thou forsaken me?" (Matthew 27:46), Jesus was expressing the profound loneliness of bearing the sins of the world. But through it all, He trusted in the Father's presence. In this way, the Savior understands our loneliness intimately, and He is able to reach into our moments of isolation with compassion, offering us the comfort that only He can provide.

When we are overwhelmed by loneliness, the Savior speaks to our hearts with words of love and reassurance. Isaiah 41:10 gives us this comforting promise: "Fear thou not; for I am with thee: be not dismayed; for I am thy God: I will strengthen thee; yea, I will help thee; yea, I will uphold thee with the right hand of my righteousness." The Savior's presence is our strength in times of loneliness. He is with us to uphold us, to carry us through the dark moments when we feel like we can't go on. His presence is not just a distant idea or a fleeting feeling—it is a reality that we can rely on every day. Even when we can't feel Him, He is there, walking beside us, holding us up, and reminding us that we are never truly alone.

One of the most beautiful pictures of the Savior's presence with us is found in Psalm 23. This well-known passage begins with, "The Lord is my shepherd; I shall not want." As our Shepherd, the Savior walks with us through every valley, including the valley of loneliness. Verse 4 says, "Yea, though I walk through the valley of the shadow of death, I will fear no evil: for thou art with me; thy rod and thy staff they comfort me." In those dark valleys where loneliness seems overwhelming, the Savior is there, guiding us, protecting us, and comforting us. His rod and staff symbolize His care for us, His constant watch over us, ensuring that we are never left to face the darkness alone. The Savior doesn't just stand at a distance, watching us struggle—He walks beside us, leading us through the valley and into the light of His presence.

The Savior's presence is not just a temporary comfort—it is a permanent promise. In Deuteronomy 31:6, God promises His people, "Be strong and of a good courage, fear not, nor be afraid of them: for the Lord thy God, he it is that doth go with thee; he will not fail thee, nor forsake thee." This promise was true for the Israelites, and it is true for us today. The Savior will never forsake us, no matter how alone we may feel. He is faithful, and His love is unchanging. When we feel abandoned by others or when life's circumstances leave us feeling isolated, we can rest in the assurance that the Savior is always with us, His presence never leaving, His love never failing.

Even in our darkest moments, when we feel like no one sees us or understands what we are going through, the Savior is there, reminding us that we are never alone. In Psalm 139:7-10, we read about the inescapable presence of God: "Whither shall I go from thy spirit? or whither shall I flee from thy presence? If I ascend up into heaven, thou art there: if I make my bed in hell, behold, thou art there. If I take the wings of the morning, and dwell in the uttermost parts of the sea; even there shall thy hand lead me, and thy right hand shall hold me." No matter where we go or how far we feel from Him, the Savior is always with us. There is no place too dark, no situation too desperate, where His presence cannot reach us. He is always near, holding us, guiding us, and reminding us that we are never out of His sight.

The Savior's presence also brings peace to our troubled hearts. In John 14:27, Jesus said, "Peace I leave with you, my peace I give unto you: not as the world giveth, give I unto you. Let not your heart be troubled, neither let it be afraid." The peace that the Savior gives is not like the temporary peace the world offers—it is a deep, abiding peace that comes from knowing that He is with us, no matter what. This peace quiets the fears that arise in moments of loneliness, reminding us that we are safe in His care. When we are anxious, when we feel overwhelmed by the weight of our isolation, the Savior's peace fills our hearts and minds, calming the storm and bringing us the reassurance that we are never alone.

The Savior's reach into our loneliness is also a reminder of His desire for relationship with us. In Revelation 3:20, Jesus says, "Behold, I stand at the door, and knock: if any man hear my voice, and open the door, I will come in to him, and will sup with him, and he with me." The Savior is always seeking to draw near to us, to be in relationship with us, to walk with us in close fellowship. He doesn't just want to be a distant figure in our lives—He wants to be close, to share in our joys and our sorrows, to be our constant companion. When we open the door of our hearts to Him, we find that we are never truly alone, for He is always with us, sharing every moment of our lives.

Even when we feel disconnected from others, the Savior reminds us that we are part of His family. In Ephesians 2:19, we are told, "Now therefore ye are no more strangers and foreigners, but fellowcitizens with the saints, and of the household of God." As believers, we are part of the household of God, a family that transcends time and space. We are never truly alone because we are connected to the body of Christ, to the Savior, and to our brothers and sisters in faith. This spiritual connection reminds us that even in moments of physical isolation, we are part of something greater—a community of believers who share in the love and grace of the Savior.

The Savior's reach into our loneliness also comes with a promise of future hope. In Revelation 21:3-4, we are given a glimpse of what is to come: "And I heard a great voice out of heaven saying, Behold, the tabernacle of God is with men, and he will dwell with them, and they shall be his people, and God himself shall be with them, and be their God. And God shall wipe away all tears from their eyes; and there shall be no more death, neither sorrow, nor crying, neither shall there be any more pain: for the former things are passed away." One day, we will dwell with God face to face, and all loneliness, sorrow, and pain will be wiped away forever. Until that day, the Savior walks with us through every moment of loneliness, reminding us of the hope we have in Him and the future we will share with Him for eternity.

In conclusion, the Savior reaches into moments of loneliness to remind us that we are never alone. His presence is constant, His love is unchanging, and His peace is ever-present in our lives. No matter how isolated we may feel, the Savior is always near, walking beside us, comforting us, and reminding us that He will never leave us nor forsake us. He understands our loneliness, and He offers us the assurance that we are never truly alone, for He is with us always, even unto the end of the world. In Him, we find the peace, comfort, and companionship that our hearts long for, and in Him, we are reminded that we are loved, seen, and known by the One who holds us in His hands.

Chapter 22 - The Savior reaches into the storms of life to calm the winds and waves.

The Savior reaches into the storms of life to calm the winds and waves, offering His divine peace in the midst of chaos and fear. Life is full of storms—moments when everything feels like it's spiraling out of control, when the winds of trouble and adversity seem too strong for us to bear, and the waves of uncertainty threaten to overwhelm us. These storms come in many forms: the loss of a loved one, financial hardship, illness, broken relationships, or even moments of deep spiritual struggle. In these times, it can feel as though we are tossed about by forces too powerful for us to withstand, lost in a sea of fear and confusion. But the Savior, in His love and mercy, steps into these storms, bringing His presence and His power to still the chaos that rages around us. In Mark 4:39, we find a powerful example of His authority over the storms: "And he arose, and rebuked the wind, and said unto the sea, Peace, be still. And the wind ceased, and there was a great calm." With just a few words, Jesus calmed the storm that had terrified His disciples, showing that no matter how fierce the storm may be, it is no match for His peace. He is the Master of the storm, and when He speaks, the winds and waves obey.

The storms of life can come suddenly, without warning, leaving us feeling unprepared and vulnerable. One moment, everything seems calm, and the next, we are in the midst of a raging storm, wondering how we will survive. This was the experience of the disciples in Mark 4. They were crossing the Sea of Galilee when, out of nowhere, a violent storm arose, threatening to capsize their boat. Despite being seasoned fishermen, they were filled with fear, certain that they were about to perish. In their panic, they cried out to Jesus, who was asleep in the boat, "Master, carest thou not that we perish?" (Mark 4:38). In that moment, their fear was overwhelming, and they questioned whether Jesus even cared about what they were going through. But the Savior's response was calm and powerful. He rose, rebuked the wind, and said to the sea, "Peace, be still." Instantly, the storm stopped, and the sea became calm. The Savior's command over the storm was a reminder that He is always in control, even when we feel like everything is falling apart. He is not distant or uncaring in our struggles; He is right there with us, ready to bring peace to the storms in our lives.

The Savior's presence in the storm is a source of comfort and assurance. Just as He was with the disciples in their storm, He is with us in ours. Even when it feels like we are alone in the midst of our struggles, the Savior is in the boat with us, never leaving our side. In Isaiah 43:2, God gives us this comforting promise: "When thou passest through the waters, I will be with thee; and through the rivers, they shall not overflow thee." The Savior does not promise that we will never face storms, but He does promise that He will be with us in them. The waters will not overwhelm us, the waves will not sweep us away, because He is there, holding us steady, keeping us safe. His presence is our anchor in the storm, giving us the strength to endure and the hope that the storm will pass.

Storms in life often cause us to question our faith, to wonder why we are going through such difficulties, and to doubt whether we will ever find peace again. But the Savior reaches into these moments of doubt and fear, reminding us that He is our refuge and strength. Psalm 46:1 declares, "God is our refuge and strength, a very present help in trouble." He is not a distant or indifferent God; He is a very present help, always near, always ready to calm the storms in our hearts and minds. When we feel overwhelmed by the chaos around us, we can turn to Him, knowing that He is our refuge, our place of safety and peace. In Him, we find the strength to face the storm, not because of our own abilities, but because of His power and His presence with us.

The Savior's ability to calm the storms of life is not just about changing our external circumstances—it's about bringing peace to our hearts, even when the storm continues to rage. In John 14:27, Jesus gives us this powerful promise: "Peace I leave with you, my peace I give unto you: not as the world giveth, give I unto you. Let not your heart be troubled, neither let it be afraid." The peace that the Savior offers is not like the temporary peace the world gives. It is a deep, abiding peace that remains with us, even in the midst of the storm. It is the kind of peace that quiets our fears and calms our anxieties, reminding us that no matter what we are facing, we are safe in His hands. This peace doesn't always mean that the storm will end immediately, but it does mean that we can have calm in our hearts, knowing that the Savior is in control.

When the Savior reaches into our storms, He does more than just calm the winds and waves—He transforms us in the process. Storms have a way of revealing what is in our hearts, exposing our fears, our doubts, and our need for control. But when we invite the Savior into the storm, He uses it as an opportunity to deepen our faith, to teach us to trust Him more fully, and to draw us closer to Him. In Romans 5:3-4, we are reminded that trials and storms in life are not without purpose: "And not only so, but we glory in tribulations also: knowing that tribulation worketh patience; and patience, experience; and experience, hope." The storms we face are not meaningless—they are opportunities for growth. When the Savior reaches into our storms, He doesn't just bring peace to the situation; He brings transformation to our hearts. He teaches us patience, deepens our faith, and fills us with hope, knowing that He is working all things together for our good.

The Savior's reach into the storms of life is also a reminder of His power and authority over all things. In Matthew 28:18, Jesus declares, "All power is given unto me in heaven and in earth." There is nothing in this world, no storm, no trial, no difficulty, that is beyond His control. When the winds of life feel too strong, when the waves of trouble feel too high, we can rest in the knowledge that the Savior has all power and authority. He is able to calm the storm with just a word, and He is able to carry us through the storm with His mighty hand. Nothing is too difficult for Him, and nothing can separate us from His love and care.

Even in the midst of the most violent storms, the Savior's love for us remains constant. In Romans 8:38-39, we are given this powerful assurance: "For I am persuaded, that neither death, nor life, nor angels, nor principalities, nor powers, nor things present, nor things to come, nor height, nor depth, nor any other creature, shall be able to separate us from the love of God, which is in Christ Jesus our Lord." The storms of life cannot separate us from the Savior's love. No matter how fierce the storm may be, His love remains unshakable, unbreakable, and ever-present. His love is the anchor that holds us steady, the foundation that keeps us from being swept away by the troubles of this world.

When the Savior calms the storms of life, He also brings healing to the wounds that the storm has caused. Storms can leave us feeling broken, weary, and scarred, but the Savior's touch brings restoration and healing. In Psalm 147:3, we are reminded of His healing power: "He healeth the broken in heart, and bindeth up their wounds." The Savior doesn't just calm the storm and walk away—He stays with us, tending to the wounds the storm has left behind. He heals our broken hearts, restores our strength, and helps us to move forward with renewed hope and faith. His healing touch is gentle and compassionate, offering us the comfort we need to recover from the storms we have faced.

The Savior's reach into the storms of life is not limited by time, distance, or circumstance. No matter where we are, no matter how fierce the storm may be, He is always near, always ready to calm the winds and waves. In Psalm 107:29, we are given this beautiful picture of His power: "He maketh the storm a calm, so that the waves thereof are still." The Savior's ability to calm the storm is not just a distant hope—it is a present reality. When we call out to Him in the midst of the storm, He hears us, and He responds with His peace and His power. He may not always remove the storm immediately, but He will always bring His presence into the storm, giving us the strength to endure and the hope that the storm will eventually pass.

In the end, the Savior's reach into the storms of life points us to the ultimate hope we have in Him—that one day, all storms will cease, and we will live in perfect peace with Him forever. In Revelation 21:4, we are given a glimpse of this future hope: "And God shall wipe away all tears from their eyes; and there shall be no more death, neither sorrow, nor crying, neither shall there be any more pain: for the former things are passed away." One day, the storms of this life will be no more. The winds and waves that have battered us will be stilled forever, and we will dwell in the presence of the Savior, where there is no more pain, no more sorrow, and no more fear. Until that day, we can trust that the Savior is with us in every storm, bringing His peace, His comfort, and His strength.

In conclusion, the Savior reaches into the storms of life to calm the winds and waves, offering us His peace, His presence, and His power in the midst of our struggles. No matter how fierce the storm may be, the Savior is in control, and He is always near, ready to speak peace into our lives. He does not leave us to face the storm alone—He is with us, holding us steady, calming our fears, and reminding us that His love and care are constant. In Him, we find the strength to endure the storm, the hope that the storm will pass, and the assurance that

His peace is greater than any chaos we face. As we trust in Him, we can rest in the knowledge that the Savior is the Master of the storm, and He will bring us safely through to the other side.

Chapter 23 - The Savior reaches into eternity to secure our place with Him forever.

The Savior reaches into eternity to secure our place with Him forever, offering us a hope that stretches beyond the boundaries of this life and into the endless glory of eternity with God. In a world where everything seems temporary and fleeting, where life is filled with uncertainty, pain, and loss, the promise of eternity with the Savior shines like a bright beacon of hope, reminding us that this world is not our final home and that our lives are part of a much greater story—one that doesn't end with death but continues forever in the presence of our loving Creator. Jesus came not only to give us abundant life here on earth, but also to secure for us an eternal home in heaven, a place where we will dwell with Him in perfect peace, joy, and love for all of eternity. In John 14:2-3, the Savior reassures us of this incredible promise: "In my Father's house are many mansions: if it were not so, I would have told you. I go to prepare a place for you. And if I go and prepare a place for you, I will come again, and receive you unto myself; that where I am, there ye may be also." These words from Jesus fill our hearts with hope, knowing that He has gone ahead of us to prepare a place for us in His Father's house, a place where we will be with Him forever.

The promise of eternity is not just a distant hope for the future—it is a reality that gives meaning and purpose to our lives today. When the Savior reaches into eternity to secure our place with Him, He invites us to live with the assurance that our future is secure, no matter what happens in this life. In 1 Peter 1:3-4, we are reminded of the inheritance that awaits us: "Blessed be the God and Father of our Lord Jesus Christ, which according to his abundant mercy hath begotten us again unto a lively hope by the resurrection of Jesus Christ from the dead, to an inheritance incorruptible, and undefiled, and that fadeth not away, reserved in heaven for you." Our inheritance in Christ is incorruptible and undefiled, and it will never fade away. This eternal inheritance is kept safe for us in heaven, and it is guaranteed by the Savior's own death and resurrection. Because of Jesus, we can live each day with the confidence that our future is secure, that no matter what trials or challenges we face, nothing can take away the eternal life that He has promised us.

The Savior's reach into eternity transforms the way we view life and death. Without the hope of eternity, death can seem like the ultimate defeat, the end of all that we know and love. But through the Savior, death has been defeated, and it is no longer something to be feared. In 1 Corinthians 15:55-57, the apostle Paul writes, "O death, where is thy sting? O grave, where is thy victory? The sting of death is sin; and the strength of sin is the law. But thanks be to God, which giveth us the victory through our Lord Jesus Christ." Because of Jesus, death has lost its sting, and the grave has lost its victory. The Savior's death and resurrection have conquered sin and death once and for all, securing for us the victory that allows us to look beyond the grave and into the glory of eternity with Him. This victory is not something we could have achieved on our own—it is a gift of grace, freely given to us through the Savior's sacrifice on the cross.

When the Savior reaches into eternity to secure our place with Him, He offers us the hope of eternal life—a life that is free from pain, sorrow, and suffering. Revelation 21:4 gives us a glimpse of this glorious future: "And God shall wipe away all tears from their eyes; and there shall be no more death, neither sorrow, nor crying, neither shall there be any more pain: for the former things are passed away." In eternity, all the brokenness of this world will be gone. The pain we experience, the tears we shed, the sorrows we carry—all of it will be wiped away in the presence of the Savior. This is the hope we cling to, especially in moments of deep grief and suffering. When life feels overwhelming and the burdens of this world feel too heavy to bear, the promise of eternity reminds us that there is a day coming when all of this will be made right. The Savior's reach into eternity ensures that we will be with Him in a place where there is no more death, no more pain, and no more heartache—only perfect peace and joy in His presence forever.

Eternity with the Savior is not just about escaping the trials of this world—it is about being in perfect, unbroken fellowship with God. From the beginning of time, humanity was created to be in relationship with God, but sin severed that relationship, separating us from the fullness of His presence. But through the Savior's death and resurrection, that relationship has been restored, and in eternity, we will experience the fullness of that relationship in ways we can only imagine. In Revelation 22:3-4, we are given a picture of this perfect fellowship: "And there shall be no more curse: but the throne of God and of the Lamb shall be in it; and his servants shall serve him: And they shall see his face; and his name shall be in their foreheads." In eternity, we will see the Savior face to face, and we will dwell with Him forever. The separation caused by sin will be gone, and we will live in the light of His presence for all of eternity, serving Him, worshiping Him, and experiencing the fullness of His love and glory.

The Savior's reach into eternity also reminds us that our lives here on earth are not the end of the story. We are not just living for the temporary things of this world—we are living for the eternal. In 2 Corinthians 4:17-18, Paul writes, "For our light affliction, which is but for a moment, worketh for us a far more exceeding and eternal weight of glory; while we look not at the things which are seen, but at the things which are not seen: for the things which are seen are temporal; but the things which are not seen are eternal." The trials and afflictions we face in this life are temporary, but the glory that awaits us in eternity is beyond anything we can comprehend. The Savior calls us to fix our eyes on the eternal, to live with the knowledge that the things of this world are passing away, but the life He offers us is everlasting. When we live with eternity in mind, it changes the way we approach life. We no longer live for the fleeting pleasures or successes of this world, but for the eternal rewards that come from knowing and serving the Savior.

The hope of eternity with the Savior also gives us courage to face the challenges of this life. In John 16:33, Jesus encourages His disciples with these words: "These things I have spoken unto you, that in me ye might have peace. In the world ye shall have tribulation: but be of good cheer; I have overcome the world." The Savior never promised that this life would be free from trials, but He did promise that He has overcome the world. Because of His victory, we can face the storms of life with confidence, knowing that no matter what we go through, our place in eternity with Him is secure. This hope gives us strength to persevere, to endure suffering, and to remain faithful, knowing that the Savior has already secured the victory and that one day, we will share in His glory forever.

The Savior's reach into eternity is also a reminder that our salvation is secure, not because of anything we have done, but because of His grace. In John 10:28-29, Jesus gives us this assurance: "And I give unto them eternal life; and they shall never perish, neither shall any man pluck them out of my hand. My Father, which gave them me, is greater than all; and no man is able to pluck them out of my Father's hand." When the Savior reaches into eternity to secure our place with Him, He holds us in His hands, and nothing can take us away from Him. Our salvation is not dependent on our ability to hold on to Him, but on His ability to hold on to us. This gives us incredible peace, knowing that our place in eternity is not something we have to earn or fight for—it is a gift of grace, guaranteed by the Savior's love and power.

Eternity with the Savior is not just a promise for the distant future—it is something we begin to experience now, through our relationship with Him. In John 17:3, Jesus defines eternal life in these words: "And this is life eternal, that they might know thee the only true God, and Jesus Christ, whom thou hast sent." Eternal life is not just about living forever—it's about knowing the Savior, experiencing His presence, and walking in relationship with Him. This is something we can experience here and now, as we grow in our knowledge of Him and live in the light of His love. The Savior's reach into eternity begins the moment we place our faith in Him, and from that moment on, we are invited to live in the reality of His eternal life, both now and forever.

In conclusion, the Savior reaches into eternity to secure our place with Him forever, offering us a hope that transcends the challenges and pains of this life. His death and resurrection have defeated sin and death, guaranteeing us an eternal home in His presence, where there is no more pain, no more sorrow, and no more death. This promise of eternity gives us peace, strength, and courage as we navigate the storms of life, knowing that our future is secure in His hands. Through His grace, we are invited into a relationship with Him that begins now and lasts forever. In the Savior, we find the assurance that we will dwell with Him in perfect peace, joy, and love for all of eternity, and this is the hope that sustains us as we journey through this life.

Conclusion

As we reach the conclusion of "The Reach That Restores: Christ's Love for the Broken," we are reminded that Christ's love, the same love that healed our hearts and brought us back from the depths of brokenness, is not a stagnant force—it is a living, breathing reality that moves us forward with purpose. Christ's reach did not stop the moment He restored us; it continues to transform us, and through us, it reaches out to a world still shrouded in pain, darkness, and despair. As Christians, we are called to carry the light of this love into every corner of our lives, letting it flow from us as naturally as a river flows to the sea. We are not simply recipients of grace—we are vessels of it, chosen to reflect His love, mercy, and compassion in our everyday interactions. This journey of restoration is not a destination we arrive at; it is a continuous, daily invitation to be reshaped into Christ's likeness, knowing that every time we stumble, His reach is there to catch us and lift us up again. Now, we must extend this grace to others, to those who feel beyond repair, beyond love, and beyond hope, because we have seen firsthand that no one is beyond the reach of the Saviour. The Christian's calling is to embody the same relentless, restoring love that touched us, to walk beside the broken, to speak words of life into despair, and to show, through our actions and our presence, that Jesus is still actively pursuing, healing, and restoring all who will come to Him. We are to go into the world not as perfect saints but as restored souls, bearing the marks of His grace, and extending His compassion to those who need it most. As we continue on this journey, may we always remember that the reach that restored us will never stop, and neither should we. We press on, fueled by His love, carrying the message of hope and healing to the ends of the earth, knowing that every act of kindness, every word of encouragement, every hand extended in love can become the very vessel through which Christ continues His restorative work in a broken and hurting world.

Don't miss out!

Visit the website below and you can sign up to receive emails whenever Joshua Rhoades publishes a new book. There's no charge and no obligation.

https://books2read.com/r/B-A-AJLBB-GKLDF

BOOKS 2 READ

Connecting independent readers to independent writers.

Did you love *The Reach That Restores Christ Love For The Broken*? Then you should read *A Christmas Journey of Faith*[1] by Joshua Rhoades!

[2]

In "A Christmas Journey of Faith", join four friends—Jake, Emma, Max, and Maya—on a thrilling time-travel adventure. When they discover a mysterious time machine hidden in an old shed, they embark on an incredible journey that takes them over 2,000 years into the past to witness the most important event in history: the birth of Jesus Christ. But this journey isn't just about seeing the past—it's about learning timeless lessons of faith, trust, and courage.

As they travel back to the time of Mary and Joseph, the friends witness the Christmas story unfold. From the angel Gabriel's visit to Mary to the long journey to Bethlehem and the miraculous birth of Jesus in a humble stable, they find themselves in the heart of the greatest miracle. They stand in awe as the shepherds receive the good news from the angels, follow the star with the wise men, and learn how Mary and Joseph trusted God's plan, even when it was difficult.

---

1. https://books2read.com/u/bWA9Qz

2. https://books2read.com/u/bWA9Qz

Each step of their journey shows how faith in God can guide us through life's challenges. The friends learn that Christmas isn't about presents or decorations, but about the gift of Jesus, who came to bring peace, love, and hope to the world. As they experience these incredible events, they realize that God's love and salvation are for everyone—rich or poor, young or old.

"A Christmas Journey of Faith" is a heartwarming story that reminds readers of all ages to trust God's plan and embrace the true meaning of Christmas. Through the eyes of Jake, Emma, Max, and Maya, readers will be inspired to live out the message of salvation and faith that Jesus brought to the world.